Andy Stephenson not only understands the importance of investing in younger generations, but he lives out the words in these pages so well. Anyone who takes the time to read these truths, biblical study merged with Andy's experience and insight, will be spurred on to deeper faith in the future generations. Read and be encouraged to pass the baton.

—Chris Tomlin, Contemporary Christian worship artist, Grammy and Dove award winner

The stakes couldn't be higher. Church attendance is declining and young people are abandoning the faith of their parents in increasing numbers. If the church is to continue to be effective in making disciples of all nations, it must "raise up a new generation of Christ-centered leaders." In his book *Smooth Hand Offs*, Andy Stephenson lays out a practical plan to do just that, a plan that is based on a solid Biblical foundation and years of practical experience. I commend his book to you.

—Bob Russell, Retired Senior Minister, Southeast Christian Church, Louisville, Kentucky

I believe all of us can think back to persons who were influential in our life's journey. Every person has both positive and negative influences as they mature and grow. The hope and the desire for the Christian is to be a positive influence and influence many persons for the sake of the kingdom. Andy Stephenson has not only lived the essence of this book, but he has instilled within others the value associated with being a positive role model and mentor. The practical helps included in the book will assist you in passing the faith along. It is worth the read.

—Dr. Ron Duncan, General Director,
Church of God Ministries

Dr. Andy Stephenson, a champion for youth, is a virtuoso in the field of training youth leaders to maximize their serve. His extensive youth ministry experience and passion to generate authentic life-change in the lives of the young provides a deep well from which he draws critical insight revealed in *Smooth Hand Offs: Passing the Baton of Faith to the Next Generations*. This timely, forward-looking work is a must-read for any critical thinker intent on leaving a legacy of influence that impacts generations.

—Steve Fitzhugh, National Speaker;
President, PowerMoves; Former NFL Player;
National Spokesperson for FCA's One Way 2 Play Program.

Andy is all about preparing the next generation. For years we have witnessed his tireless dedication to encouraging and equipping the next generation to make their faith their own, to live it out and pass it on. Andy is so gifted in the area of surrounding himself with capable servants and empowering them do the work God has for them. You'd never know he had such leadership skills because his biceps are so puny compared to ours!

—**Tommy & Eddie, The Skit Guys**

Andy Stephenson has seen the results of failing to successfully train the next generation in the Christian faith. His personal discipline and attitude inspire trust and faith, which are attractive and contagious. Andy rejects instant gratification, replacing it with obedience, discipline and accountability. He gives the reader practical directions for passing along authentic Christian faith. This book speaks to one of the truly great needs in today's church. It is excellent for helping those in the church know how to pass their faith on to other generations.

—**Arlo Newell, Editor in Chief, Retired, Warner Press, Inc.**

The conversation of the next generation is a critical one. Andy Stephenson gets beyond discussion and gives very practical steps to implementing the vital steps to pass on the faith. This is a task that we must give our attention and focus to. Andy is a seasoned leader with a passion to equip leaders to do the right things. He has made a clear challenge that all leaders of the next generation must read!

—Bubba Thurman, Executive Pastor of Family and Student Ministries, Lakepointe Church, Rockwall, Texas

Andy Stephenson challenges us to think about our personal role in reaching a generation for Christ and gives a practical focused goal to ensure real spiritual transformation takes place in the lives of students. In *Smooth Hand Offs*, Andy focuses on the main goal—Jesus' model for us to follow—and gives practical ways to disciple and train the next generation of Christ followers.

—Bo Boshers
President of Lead222 and Former Executive Director of Student Ministries at Willow Creek Community Church and the Willow Creek Association

I've had the privilege to know and participate in student ministry with Andy Stephenson for more than a decade. From day one I knew he had a 2 Timothy 2:2 heart. He knows the power of multiplication in the spiritual world and has committed his life to not talking about it but doing it. That's why *Smooth Hand Offs* is so powerful. Andy is not only sharing what he's learned, but he is entrusting those truths to us so we can tell others.

—Allen Weed, President, Interlinc

smooth hand offs
passing the baton of faith to the next generations

andy stephenson, phd

Warner Press
Anderson, Indiana

Coordinator of Publishing & Creative Services
Church of God Ministries, Inc.
PO Box 2420
Anderson, IN 46018-2420
800-848-2464
www.chog.org

To purchase additional copies of this book, to inquire about distribution, and for all other sales-related matters, please contact:

 Warner Press, Inc.
PO Box 2499
Anderson, IN 46018-2499
800-741-7721
www.warnerpress.org

All Scripture quotations, unless otherwise indicated, are taken from the Holy Bible, New International Version˙. NIV˙. Copyright © 1973, 1978, 1984 by Biblica. Used by permission of Zondervan. All rights reserved.

Free online study guide available at http://alturl.com/m44ty.

ISBN-13: 978-1-59317-593-1

Printed in the United States of America.

LSI

This book is dedicated to my grandfather, Rev. George R. Harrington (1908–2008), who was passing the baton until his death at ninety-nine and for whom passing the baton was as natural as breathing, and to my parents, who continue to model what it means to pass it well to so many.

Contents

Preface xi

Acknowledgments xiii

Chapter 1: The Race: Situation Critical, Today and Yesterday 1

Chapter 2: The Baton Drop 11

Chapter 3: We All Run on the Same Track 21

Chapter 4: Raising Up a Generation Who GETS IT 29

Chapter 5: Where Are the Runners Who Finish Strong? 43

Chapter 6: Following the Course Map 53

Chapter 7: Running a Race with Focus 63

Chapter 8: Making Smooth Hand Offs 75

Chapter 9: A Call to Church Leaders 89

Chapter 10: Race Victories 99

Appendix 113

Preface

This book is the culmination of numerous years of interaction and observation of thousands of individuals in the younger generations and of my work with leaders. This book was written, and tweaked and reworked, over the course of nine years. My prayer is that this won't be just another book you read and put on your shelf, but that you will apply what is in it, live it, loan it out for others to read, and that together we will help raise up a generation of Christ-centered leaders. My prayer is that we make smooth handoffs of the baton of faith to the generations behind us, that we are a part of the GETS IT movement, and that when they write the history books about us, they will write that we made a smooth handoff.

Andy Stephenson

Acknowledgments

Special thanks to my incredible wife Candace for all her support as I wrote this project and to my daughters Mackenzie and Morgan, who are constant reminders of the need for smooth hand offs. I can't thank my sister, Kristi Hayes; my interns Charlie Holcomb and Lainey Priddy; and my master editing mom, Georgetta Stephenson, enough for all the input and reads and rereads of the drafts of *Smooth Hand Offs*. Thank you so much for all the help and wisdom. You have so many fingerprints on this project. Special thanks to Jeannette Flynn for all the support while writing this book, to Joe Allison for all the writing advice, and to Dr. Ron Duncan for a quick conversation in a hallway years ago that helped water the seeds for this project.

Chapter One

The Race: Situation Critical, Today and Yesterday

ARE WE PASSING THE BATON WELL?

As I pulled into the church parking lot, I saw something odd in front of the entrance to the office doors. It looked like someone carrying a blanket or a sleeping bag. Had this person been sleeping in the doorway overnight? Crime was frequent in our part of town, and the church had been broken into two or three times within a span of a month or two. We had to keep the doors locked during the day and have an alarm system for the safety of our staff. I had to be careful going out to my car when I worked late at night. Yet, in all my years here, I didn't remember anyone sleeping at the door when I pulled up for work.

It was one of my youth ministry students, who had spent the night with his girlfriend outside the church building. He came from a very troubled home, so I wasn't too surprised at this behavior. His parents didn't keep close tabs on his whereabouts or behavior; I'm not sure they really cared. Without someone in his life who genuinely cared about him, he didn't stand a chance of becoming a mature Christian.

On the other hand, there were some students in our group who seemed certain to follow in the faith footsteps of their parents. Their parents were elders or strong lay leaders in the church, and they seemed to really care. Their students came to almost every youth event and regularly attended worship services; some were even student leaders. Yet I remember asking the daughter of one of our church elders about some basic—I mean *very* basic—tenants of the Christian faith and she couldn't answer me. I found this wasn't uncommon for many of the students who had grown up in the

1

church. Many had very little biblical knowledge; others had some or a lot of knowledge, but there was little evidence of Christian faith in their everyday lives.

George Barna's current research validates the accuracy of my casual research. Barna found that 61% of today's young adults had been actively involved in the church during their teen years, but were now spiritually disengaged (i.e., not actively attending church, reading the Bible, or praying).[1]

We may think of several explanations. Perhaps that 61% attended churches without strong pastoral leadership or the churches really didn't have strong educational programs. I would disagree. After working with hundreds of youth leaders and congregations over the years, I would say that many good pastors, strong teachers, and carefully planned programs have still turned out many students in that faltering 61%. I, myself, have had more students than I want to admit who have been part of that 61% in the ministries I have been a part of.

We may also try to excuse ourselves by saying that times are just more difficult today. Just look at some of the recent news stories: "Police say a 15-year-old Boy Scout charged with killing his parents and two younger brothers shot them as they slept, then returned a day later after spending time with friends to stage the discovery of their deaths. Nicholas was working toward becoming an Eagle Scout, and had built a prayer garden at his church to meet one of the requirements."[2] "Jeff Weise, 16, killed his grandfather and companion, then arrived at school where he killed a teacher, a security guard, 5 students, and finally himself, leaving a total of 10 dead."[3]

---

1. Barna Group, "Most Twenty Somethings Put Christianity on the Shelf Following Spiritually Active Teen Years," Barna.org, September 11, 2006, http://www.barna.org/barna-update/article/16-teensnext-gen/147-most-twentysomethings-put-christianity-on-the-shelf-following-spiritually-active-teen-years?q=teens+church.

2. CBS News, "Cops: Boy Scout Killed Parents, 2 Brothers," CBS Interactive, February 11, 2009, http://www.cbsnews.com/stories/2008/02/04/national/main3788009.shtml?source=RSSattr=HOME_3788009.

3. Infoplease, "Time Line of Worldwide School Shootings," Pearson Education, last modified March 10, 2012, http://www.infoplease.com/ipa/A0777958.html.

The nightly network news and newspaper headlines scream that these are crazy times. Students today are continuously exposed to violence, sex, dishonesty, and other kinds of moral corruption. It often seems overwhelming.

Some of us adults in the church like to talk about the "good old days" when things were supposedly better. Yet, were things really that much better in the good old days? Has our culture reached a new low of human morality, or are we repeating a cycle found hundreds of years ago? We could argue that belief systems are different than they were a few decades ago, especially among the younger generations and especially in the United States. On the other hand, the Bible gives us clear evidence that moral corruption and hedonistic belief systems have been popular before.

You see, the Bible doesn't hide the messiness of people's lives. On the contrary, it shows humans in all their depravity. The book of Judges describes a culture of people estimated to have lived 1,000 to 1,400 years before Christ, over three thousand years ago. These people didn't have electricity, so there were no microwaves, text messaging, iPods, cell phones, televisions, cinemas, radios, or the Internet. What could they possibly have in common with us? While the people described by the book of Judges lacked the conveniences we have to make life easier, they had values and beliefs quite similar to those that shape our culture today.

In recent years, we have seen an outpouring of books on the post-modern generation. For our purposes, we will define a *postmodern* culture as one in which individuals create their own truth rather than discovering it. This is a significant break from modernism's belief that truth originates outside of one's self.[4] When each person determines his or her own truth, it is a subjective process with numerous problems. I determine truth according to what benefits me, regardless of how it affects you. No matter how altruistic we think we are, deep down we are self-serving. So what I think is right for me might not be right for you and actually may harm you. If there isn't an objective

---

4. George Barna, *Real Teens* (Ventura, CA: Regal, 2001), 94–97.

standard of truth, society runs into trouble quickly. Subjective truth always gets us into trouble. In reality, laws become useless if subjective truth is pushed to its extreme.

Did you ever have a teacher or professor who awarded grades on the basis of who you were rather than on the quality of work you did? I used to have a professor who favored pretty females. He treated them differently than the rest of us in class. Was it right? Of course not, it was subjective. But if we take the postmodern paradigm to its fullest extent, we can't criticize this approach. We can't criticize the atrocities of Adolf Hitler if truth is subjective, because those actions seemed right to him. Anyone with a simple conscience knows that Hitler's actions were terribly wrong and inhumane, but you can see quickly that the philosophy that "all truth is relative" runs into trouble very quickly.

As I noted earlier, this postmodern philosophy is not a new way of thinking. The Bible describes similar tenets in a culture that existed over three thousand years ago.

The book of Judges tells of a time when Israelites and Canaanites lived together in the same land. The Israelites were instructed to serve and obey one God; he was to be their objective authority. Yet the Israelites often adopted the beliefs of the Canaanites. The Canaanite pantheon was so large and diverse that a person could do anything and still be obeying at least one of the many Canaanite gods. For this reason, Canaanites believed everyone could look out for themselves, set their own rules, and still meet some legitimate religious requirements. It was a me-first mentality.[5]

The Canaanites could have said, "What's right for you might not be right for me," or, "I will choose my own spiritual beliefs, so don't push your beliefs on me." Read those sentences again and see if they don't sound familiar.

Fast forward three thousand years to today and consider our next generation of young people—a generation that has been called the

---

5. *Life Application Study Bible* (Wheaton, IL: Tydale House Publishers, 1988), 376.

millennials, Gen Y, or the mosaic generation. George Barna coined the term *mosaic* because

- ▶ their lifestyles are an eclectic combination of traditional and alternative activities;

- ▶ they are the first generation among whom a majority will exhibit a nonlinear style of thinking—a mosaic, connect-the-dots-however-you-choose approach;

- ▶ their core values are the result of a cut-and-paste mosaic of feelings, facts, principles, experiences, and lessons; and

- ▶ their central spiritual tenets are a customized blend of multiple faith views and religious practices.[6]

Two national surveys conducted by The Barna Group, one directed toward adults and another toward teenagers, asked if people believed moral absolutes are unchanging or relative to the circumstances. "64% of adults said truth is always relative to the person and their situation, not absolute and unchanging." Among teenagers, only 6% said moral truth is absolute and unchanging. Even more alarming, only 9% of teens who claim to be born-again Christians believe in moral absolutes. "By far the most common basis for moral decision-making was doing whatever feels right or comfortable in a situation. Nearly four out of ten teens (38%) and three out of ten adults (31%) described that as their primary consideration." Among adults, 13% said they based their moral decision making on principles taught in the Bible. Among teenagers, the number was even lower: 7%.[7]

Look at it this way: Suppose you were playing soccer with a group of teenagers and only one player on the team of eleven believed that you had to kick the ball through the goal in order to score. That

---

6. Barna, *Real Teens*, 17.

7. Barna Group. "Americans Are Most Likely to Base Truth on Feelings," Barna.org, February 12, 2002, http://www.barna.org/barna-update/article/5-barna-update/67-americans-are-most-likely-to-base-truth-on-feelings?q=moral+decision-making.

would be a problem. According to the research, only one player on the entire team of eleven would say that God's truth is absolute and unchanging. This would be true regardless of whether you assembled a soccer team of all Christian or all unchristian students. Barna's research shows that only one player on either of these teams would believe in the concept of absolute right and wrong.

My experience tends to confirm these statistics. God often places interesting people in my path on my travels. On a flight to Chicago, I sat next to a twenty-three-year-old woman who was a national representative for a sorority. She had just graduated from college, and her job during the next year was to travel around the country, visiting sororities to see if they were maintaining the standards of the organization. She was lively and extremely extroverted. As they would say down South, she was a "talker." She talked the whole way. After learning a little about her, I got to the question that I often ask when I want to talk about Christ. I asked if she had any spiritual beliefs. She readily responded like a typical postmodern: She said she thinks all religions have parts that are good, so she takes different parts of them to live by.

It was typical of hundreds of conversations we could have had with people of her generation. They have a mix-and-match approach to spirituality. However, in the Bible I find no option to mix and match. First John 5:11–12, says, "And this is the testimony: God has given us eternal life, and this life is in his Son. He who has the Son has life, he who does not have the Son of God does not have life." In John 14:6 we read, "Jesus answered, 'I am the way and the truth and the life. No one comes to the Father except through me.'" Acts 4:12 indicates that "salvation is found in no one else, for there is no other name under heaven given to men by which we must be saved."

You can't be neutral about who Jesus is. There really isn't an in-between. Either he was who he said he was—the son of God and the only way to God—or, as former atheist C.S. Lewis said,

> A man who was merely a man and said the sort of things Jesus said would not be a great moral teacher. He would either be a

lunatic—on the level of a man who says he is a poached egg—or else he would be the Devil of Hell. You must make your choice. Either this man was, and is, the Son of God: Or else He is a madman...or something worse. You can shut Him up for a fool; you can spit at Him and kill Him as a demon; or you can fall at His feet and call Him Lord and God. But let us not come with any patronizing nonsense about His being a great human teacher. He has not left that open to us."[8]

Those who have no relationship with Christ are confused, but they are not the only ones. Even teenagers in our churches who claim to follow Christ are confused.

I was speaking at a youth convention of a conservative Christian group and had made a very small reference in my message about how God was more interested in having a relationship with us than about having us do religion. I stressed that God doesn't call us to a religion and a bunch of dos and don'ts, but to a relationship. I mentioned that we didn't have to kneel a certain direction on a certain mat and pray a certain number of times a day, or follow an eightfold path of enlightenment to get to God. Christianity is all about having a relationship with God, not about earning our way to God.

After my message, a young lady approached me in the hall and said, "I don't appreciate the off-handed remark you made about Islam." Since my reference to Islam was very brief and obscure, I should have thanked her for staying awake and listening so closely! Instead, I assured her that the Bible says Jesus Christ is the only way to God. After a few moments of conversation, she stormed off very angrily, saying that I just wouldn't "get it." She was trying to convince me that there are many different paths to God, and we should be willing to try them all.

A few days earlier, I had listened to a presentation in a large vibrant youth ministry in a strong evangelical church as their students tried to explain why Jesus Christ is the only way to a genuine rela-

---

8. C. S. Lewis, *Mere Christianity*, rev. ed. (New York: Macmillan/Collier, 1952), 55.

tionship with God. They struggled to articulate it, but they couldn't. Some of these students had grown up in the church. As mentioned earlier, Barna's research indicates this isn't just an issue for those outside the church; it's an issue for those inside the church as well.[9]

Relativism of belief isn't the only thing we have in common with the Canaanites of three thousand years ago. Sexual immorality is another. The Canaanite culture in which the Israelites lived was very sensual in nature. Sexual permissiveness was a way of life. It was everywhere. The Canaanite religion worshiped immoral deities and prostitute goddesses. El was thought to be chief deity, and his son Baal was the most significant deity in the Canaanite religion. Baal was believed to have dethroned his father and murdered his own daughter and son. Baal was also believed to control all forms of reproduction. There were also female deities, such as Ashtaroth (the goddess of fertility, love, and war) and Anath (referred to as the queen of heaven). The prescribed worship of these Canaanite gods included sacred prostitution, and their mythical stories described acts of extreme brutality and immorality. Sex orgies and temple prostitution were common parts of the worship experience.[10]

Compare that to our present-day culture. How many primetime television shows or popular movies can you watch without some sexual content or innuendos? From sitcoms to reality shows, sexual lingo, sexual escapades, and scanty dress are a major part of television programming. Louis Harris and Associates estimates that the average television viewer witnesses 14,000 sexual events annually.[11] A study conducted a few years ago indicated that nearly 8 in 10 (77%) primetime television shows include sexual content, averag-

9. Barna Group. "Americans Are Most Likely to Base Truth on Feelings," Barna.org, February 12, 2002, http://www.barna.org/barna-update/article/5-barna-update/67-americans-are-most-likely-to-base-truth-on-feelings?q=moral+decision-making.

10. Leon Wood, *Distressing Days of the Judges* (Grand Rapids, MI: Zondervan, 1975), 143–44. James L. Kelso, *Archaeology and the Ancient Testament* (Grand Rapids, MI: Zondervan, 1968), 55.

11. David G. Myers and Martin E. Marty, *The American Paradox: Spiritual Hunger in an Age of Plenty* (New Haven, CT: Yale University Press, 2000), 214.

ing 5.9 sexual scenes per hour. Expanding beyond prime time, the research indicated two-thirds (68%) of all television shows include some talk about sex.[12]

In our current culture, references to sex are everywhere. You can hardly watch a sporting event on television with your son or daughter without having to change the channel during the commercials because of sexually charged content. You see it on billboards while driving down the interstate. You see sexual content plastered on posters and advertisements while walking through the mall. Sex is everywhere. Clothing companies that market to teens and young adults have catalogs that look like soft porn. In some stores, male and female models—often scantily dressed—greet shoppers. It is often said that sex sells, and marketers believe it. Almost everywhere you look in our present culture, there is some connection to sex. Our culture is obsessed with sex, much like the Canaanite culture over three thousand years ago where sexual obsession was a major driver. How close the past and the present parallel one another!

But there's more. Research shows that even the belief systems of younger generations in our churches are moving farther from what the Bible teaches. Is the church in danger of losing the next generations? If current trends are any indication, the prognosis is dim. Yet we don't have to throw in the towel just yet.

Because a culture saturated with sex and subjective religious beliefs isn't a new phenomenon, we can learn much from what happened in the past and consider how we can prepare the next generations for a different ending. In the following chapters, we will take a journey to see what track we are currently running and how we can make some intentional shifts to take the baton of faith and make a smooth handoff to the next generations.

---

12. Kaiser Family Foundation, "Number of Sexual Scenes on TV Nearly Double Since 1998," www.kff.org, November 9, 2005, http://www.kff.org/entmedia/entmedia110905nr.cfm.

Application Questions

1. Do you think the moral climate of our culture is improving or deteriorating? On what facts do you base this opinion?

2. How are the moral values of the United States today similar to those of the Canaanites over three thousand years ago?

3. Have you seen any Christians in your church or other circles of acquaintance who have ended their walk with God? Why do you think this happens?

4. Statistics show that a high percentage of young Christians leave the church or fall away from Christ entirely. How do you think we might turn this trend around?

5. What can you do personally to reverse this?

Chapter Two

The Baton Drop

PART ONE: A LOOK AT WHAT HAPPENED AFTER MOSES PASSED THE BATON TO JOSHUA

You have probably seen, in the sport of track and field, the relay race made up of four individuals who pass the baton off to each other and run a certain distance with the baton. When I was in high school, one of the track and field events I participated in was the 4 x 400-meter relay. In this relay, a team is made up of four runners. Each runner runs 400 meters, referred to as their leg, and hands over a baton to a teammate, who then begins their leg upon receiving the baton. The runners must hand off the baton within a designated section of the track and may be disqualified if the hand off is made outside the designated area, or if they drop the baton during the race. If you have ever run the relays or watched a relay race, you know that the most important component in the 4 x 400, or any other relay, is the passing of the baton from one runner to the next. This critical aspect typically determines the outcome of the race. If the baton hand off isn't made smoothly, at just the right time or in the right area, it usually costs the relay team the race. As a member of a relay team, I remember practicing hand offs over and over again. No matter how fast your team is or how great the athletes are, if you are unable to make a smooth hand off of the baton, you are likely headed for defeat.

If you watched the 2008 Summer Olympics in Beijing, you saw perfect examples of what happens when you miss the hand off. In the Olympics, you have athletes who have been practicing for years, if not all of their lives, for this moment. In the Olympic semifinals of the 4 x 100-meter relays, the USA men's team was a favorite and expected to compete for a gold medal. As the starting gun sounded, the runners were running at full speed, neck and neck for first place;

the announcers were getting excited; the fans were on their feet. I am sure the runners could only picture themselves on the podium receiving a gold medal in the next round, and then the unthinkable happened. The USA relay team, a strong favorite to compete for a gold medal, dropped the baton and was disqualified from the race. They didn't even make it to the medal round. Less than an hour later, the favored USA women's 4 x 100-meter relay team did exactly the same thing. Both teams missed the finals despite having some of the fastest runners in the world. The next night in the finals the heavily favored Jamaican women's 4 x 100 relay team did the very same thing—they dropped the baton and lost the race. If you could line all those runners up, you would see that they are some of the fastest sprinters in the world, but they lost the race because they failed to hand off the baton smoothly. No matter how fast athletes are, without a smooth pass of the baton the race is lost.

You may have never run on a relay team, but the reality is that we are all in a relay race. When we were born, we became a part of a race called life, and whether we want this responsibility or not, we will make some type of hand off to the generations that follow us. Each of us runs with a baton of faith and the responsibility that God has given us to hand it off smoothly to the next generation. Specifically, God has given us the responsibility, as his followers, to model for the younger generation how to properly run the spiritual race. Just as with a 4 x 100-meter relay, the runner handing the baton and the runner receiving the baton run a little way together in the pass. We all have a duty to train and coach those younger than us by running along beside them and by handing them the baton to carry and pass on to future generations. What kind of hand off will we make? A smooth one? An awkward one? Or worse, an unsuccessful one where the baton crashes to the ground?

The book of Judges paints a picture of the race the Israelites were running over three millenia ago. The race is in full swing and the current generation is about to get to the critical stage in the race, the place on the track where they are about to hand off the baton. What happened next is, well, very interesting and sobering. Let's enter as spectators in this great race.

The opening line of Judges says, "After the death of Joshua...." Joshua, what type of runner was he? Exodus 24:13 indicates that Joshua was Moses's aide: "Then Moses set out with Joshua his aide, and Moses went up on the mountain of God." We find in Numbers 11:28 that Joshua had been Moses's aide or apprentice since his youth. Joshua was coached by Moses and had been on quite a run with Moses, not just a sprint, but a marathon. Joshua had seen the ten plagues in Egypt and the Israelites delivered from slavery. He had seen the Red Sea open up and the Egyptian army swallowed up after the Israelites walked across on dry ground. He had watched God turn water from bitter to sweet. He had seen food for a group of an estimated two million people rain down from heaven on a consistent basis.

Joshua received the baton from Moses during the journey in the wilderness that should have taken only eleven days, but because of the disobedience of the people, it took forty years. He had seen Moses deal with conflict on numerous occasions. All you have to do is flip through Exodus and the book of Numbers to see that Moses dealt with conflict frequently. I am sure he heard more than once, "It seems we are walking around in circles!" Joshua had seen the earth swallow Korah and his disgruntled followers. Joshua had been by Moses's side when Moses threw down the Ten Commandments after witnessing the people who had forsaken God to worship golden calves just a short time after God had delivered them from Egypt.

Joshua was a runner who had seen Moses's face shine because of his time on the mountain with God and the direct relationship that his mentor had with the almighty. Moses had invested thousands of hours of time into Joshua, and Joshua had seen Moses's life as a godly example. For 14,600 days, Joshua had seen the example of Moses in good times and bad times, celebration and despair, conflict and peace.

Moses had been running alongside of Joshua and preparing to pass him the baton. Now we come to the critical moment, the most important part of the race, the passing of the baton. In Numbers

27:18, we find these words: "So the LORD said to Moses, 'Take Joshua son of Nun, a man in whom is the spirit, and lay your hand on him.'" Moses did as God had commanded and made the hand off.

Joshua takes the baton from Moses in his lane. The hand off is smooth. The spectators are cheering; it looks like the team is running on all cylinders. And now he starts his leg, the charge of taking around two million people who have been wanderers all their adult lives into the Promised Land. He was now leading a people who knew how to walk around in circles but weren't very good at getting anywhere. Joshua took leadership of a people who were used to moving aimlessly from here to there for years and years without ever reaching their final destination. Think about it, forty years wandering on a journey that should have taken eleven days. Perhaps this will put things into perspective next time you get lost for a few hours on the family vacation.

In Joshua 1:10–12, we find Joshua's next move. He tells the people to pack their bags because in three days they're going somewhere. Can you imagine what the Israelites must have heard? It must have been music to their ears when Joshua stood before the people and said, "We are going to a destination. A place you have been destined for all of your lives. We are crossing the Jordan and going to the place God has given us. After forty years of wandering around getting nowhere, in three days we are going to what we have been made for, the Promised Land! We aren't just running to run; we are now going to run and really get somewhere! We are going to reach a finish line."

Joshua said to the Israelites, "Get your supplies ready. Three days from now you will cross the Jordan here to go in and take possession of the land..." (Josh 1:11) Three days later, Joshua and the people went to the edge of the Jordan River. Most likely it was a large group of apprehensive people with all of their possessions, and guess what? The Jordan River was at flood stage; getting across would be nearly impossible. Yet God was in control and performed a miracle. Joshua 3:15–16 says, "As soon as the priests...reached the Jordan and their feet touched the water's edge, the water from upstream stopped flowing." God had it under control.

As we look more closely at the Israelites new leader, we find that Joshua was a brilliant military strategist—one of the "who's who" of military men of that day. Under his leadership the Israelites attacked king after king and took over territory after territory. On the west side of the Jordan alone, thirty-one kings were conquered. Under Joshua, the Hittites, Amorites, Canaanites, and a number of other -ites were defeated. Joshua was a military genius. He would have been commended for his valor and for his ability to do his job. If he had had a human supervisor, he would have always scored high marks on his job evaluations. Yet in the race of life, what constitutes success? Do accomplishments, trophies, high salaries, and decorations really mean we have done a good job? In most cultures, especially in North America, the answer would be yes.

Individualism, especially in the Western culture, is seen as strength. Some of the mottos are, "It's a dog-eat-dog world out there," and, "Do what you have to do to get ahead." Does having a lot of stuff constitute finishing well? Does having fame or a lot of accolades mean you lived life to the fullest? How many people on their deathbed have said, "I wish I would have worked harder and gotten more stuff?" What do people usually say? "I wish I would've spent more time with my family"; "I wish I wouldn't have worked so many hours"; or, "I wish I would have invested more in others." What constitutes running this race with valor? What does it mean to finish strong? In the relays, finishing strong is the last runner flawlessly receiving the baton and running like the wind. Finishing well is making the smooth hand off, running strong, and crossing that finish line.

Picking back up with our race, in chapter two of Judges, we find Joshua is now old—110 to be exact. He has helped lead the Israelites into the Promised Land, and now we come to the end of Joshua's life—the final evaluation that all of us will come to one day. On that day, all the accolades and accomplishments will be forgotten. What has Joshua done to pass the baton of faith on to the next generation? When people think of Joshua will they say, "He ran the race and passed the baton well?" Judges 2:6–8 says, "After Joshua had dismissed the Israelites, they went to take possession of the land, each to his own inheritance. The people served the LORD throughout the lifetime of Joshua and of the elders who outlived him and who had seen all the great things the LORD had done for Israel. Joshua son of Nun, the servant of the LORD, died at the age of a hundred and ten." Did you catch the key phrase: "The people served the LORD throughout the lifetime of Joshua." This is a powerful statement, but the statement in verse ten summarizes what type of hand off Joshua made to the next generation in the race of life.

Now we jump to verse ten, and put your seat belts on because this is a direction-setting epitaph: "After that whole generation had been gathered to their fathers, another generation grew up, who knew neither the LORD nor what he had done for Israel." Here we have it, the final segment of the race; God started the race and handed the baton to Moses. Moses ran the first leg of the race and handed the baton to Joshua. Joshua ran the second leg of the race, and now we get to the third leg. Joshua holds the baton. He ran a superb second leg, but he blew the hand off. The most important part of the race was before him, and Joshua dropped the baton.

PART TWO: A LOOK AT WHAT HAPPENED AFTER JOSHUA'S RUN

What happened? Joshua had such a great coach and mentor, who made a smooth hand off. How did Joshua miss it? How did an entire generation grow up not knowing the Lord or what he had done for Israel? When you study the life of Moses, you see Joshua beside him, life experience after life experience, being trained by Moses. Moses had been a godly example and intentionally invested time in Joshua. He ran alongside Joshua and made a smooth baton pass. He discipled him. He helped in his spiritual formation. Yet when you study the life of Joshua, you don't find him discipling a next-generation leader. No younger leader is mentioned as being at his side. This is major; here is a man who had seen the example Moses set for 14,600 days. He had seen Moses deal with conflict, he had seen God deliver the Israelites time after time, and he had seen Moses in times of joy and in times of sorrow. Here is a man who had been invested in for a full forty years! He had been handed the baton and instead of passing it on, he held on to it.

Because of this lack of discipleship, this unwillingness to hand over his baton and this lack of life investment, there was a huge leadership vacuum after Joshua and the elders died. It even starts in Judges 1:1 with a paradigm shift. In the past, both Moses and Joshua were God's appointed leaders. God appointed the leaders and the leaders helped guide the people. After Joshua dies holding his baton, we find the people have moved from a people that God guides directly through a God-appointed leader to a people that lead themselves.[1]

The first sentence in Judges reflects the sense of not having a smooth hand off from Joshua. The people are at a loss of what to do, so they ask God, "Who will be the first to go up and fight for us against the Canaanites?" (Judg 1:1). This starts them on a 325-year trek through six successive periods of oppression and deliverance through the careers of twelve deliverers. The Israelites would often obey God while a judge was living, and then when the judge died, they would revert back to disobeying him. A leader (judge) would deliver them, but when that person died, the leadership vacuum occurred again. There were twelve judges in 325 years, none of whom had been passed the baton and consequently had never learned how to pass it on themselves. They were leaders who never had the hand off modeled for them.

Joshua ran well, but he never made the hand off. The leaders who followed him did the same. Just as Joshua had modeled, they often ran a hard race, but they never passed the baton. Let's check out what happened at the end of their segment of the race.

In Judges 3:12, the summary statement of Othneil's hand off after his death states, "Once again the Israelites did evil in the eyes of the LORD." Then in chapter 4:1, "After Ehud died, the Israelites once again did evil in the eyes of the LORD." In Judges 6:1, after the leadership of Deborah, "again the Israelites did evil in the eyes of the LORD." And then, "No sooner had Gideon died than the Israelites

---

1. Tammi Schneider and Berit Olam, *Studies in Hebrew Narrative and Poetry* (Collegeville, MN: Liturgical Press, 2000), 2.

again prostituted themselves to the Baals" (8:33). After Tola and Jair, "again the Israelites did evil in the eyes of the LORD" (10:6). After Jephthah, Ibzan, Elon and Abdon, we read in Judges 13:1 that "again the Israelites did evil in the eyes of the LORD." After the final judge, Samson, we find the Israelites once again turning from God. After each of the twelve leaders listed in the book of Judges, the Israelites followed this pattern of turning from God. Joshua started the cycle and each judge continued it, often running a good leg of the race but missing the passing of the baton.

At the end of the book of Judges, we come to the unbelievable result of what happens when the spiritual baton is not passed on to the next generation. Without God, the people are left to their own ways. In the final chapters, we find that the wickedness among the people escalates to such a point that a woman is gang-raped by a bunch of homosexual/bisexual men and dies. Her husband then cuts her dead body into twelve pieces and sends those body parts throughout the territory of Israel. The result is a civil war in which sixty-five thousand people are killed. Now we come to the very last words in the book of Judges, the summary, the end of the story, the conclusion, the last leg of the race—the result of what happens when the spiritual baton is not passed. In Judges 21:25 are the final words: "Everyone did as he saw fit" (21:25).

No one had passed the baton, so everyone did whatever was right in his or her own eyes. They didn't know where to run or what lane to run in. It is interesting when we look at our current postmodern generation and how this language seems to fit. "Everyone did as they saw fit," or everyone decides what is right and wrong as an individual not from an outside objective God. Yet for us, there is hope. We are still in the race, and we are still running. We don't have to have a final ending like the Israelites in the book of Judges. We still have time to learn to pass the baton well.

Application Questions

1. Dr. Stephenson says, "Each of us runs with a baton of faith and the responsibility that God has given us to hand it off smoothly to the next generation." How would you apply this to yourself?

2. What were some reasons that Joshua didn't make a smooth hand off of his spiritual leadership?

3. What factors keep Christian leaders from making smooth hand offs today?

4. Which of these factors are the biggest hindrances for you?

5. When you reflect on your life, how do you assess whether you have been successful?

Chapter Three

We All Run on the Same Track

GOING DEEPER

I often find myself reading history books about people who lived years ago and making judgments about them. I especially find this true when I read about the Israelites and their journeys in Scripture, many of which seem to someone reading thousands of years later to be full of bad decisions. Yet, I have to remind myself before I go too far with that thought, we aren't much different today. Actually, we are very similar. We all run on the same oval track, running in the same direction with the same motions: we are born, run with a baton, and finally choose to hold on to the baton or pass it to the next generation and another generation takes our place.

This chapter is a little bit of a pause on our baton-passing journey to help us think more deeply and introspectively about the past, present, and future. I often am amazed at how the Israelites wandered around in the desert for forty years and never got anywhere. How did they just wander around in the same desert without getting to a destination? Before we are too hard on them, wandering and not getting anywhere may be something we can all relate to in life.

I remember a time when I was wandering. I was dropped off early in the morning on a ranch in North Texas. It was still dark out and the snow was blowing blizzard-like as I searched for the box stand I planned to sit in and observe wildlife. I had been here before, but this time the snow was so intense that I could only see about a body length in front of me. Before I knew it, I was turned around and didn't know where I was going. What I did know was that this ranch was thousands of acres and if I didn't find where I was going, I could be wandering for a long time. It was a frightening and unbelievably unnerving experience—not being able to find shelter in a blinding snowstorm and wandering around not knowing where I was.

Often we wander in our life decisions. We look for something, something that we think will fill our emptiness, but oftentimes we get to that place and it doesn't fill that void, so we start wandering and looking again, often wandering into dangerous places or territories. The Israelites had been wandering, many of them the majority of their lives, but Joshua told them that in three days they were going to make a shift.

The journey of the Israelites parallels how some of us live. So often we wander around aimlessly in the desert for months and sometimes years and it looks like we will never find our promised land, and then all of a sudden God says, just as he said to the Israelites, "Pack your bags; we are going to the Promised Land!"

You may still be in the desert waiting for the call to go to the Promised Land. I remember some seasons in my life when it felt as if I was just like the Israelites, hopelessly wandering in a place that seemed in my soul to be barren, dry, and desolate. I wondered whether there was anyone else around. God, are you there? Can you help me? I realized later that God was always there, but sometimes these wandering treks teach us much about God and ourselves. And sometimes what we thought was the Promised Land wasn't really God's best for us. Sometimes the wandering is a short season and other times it seems like it will never end. I am sure that after forty years the Israelites wondered if the wandering would ever end; but in an instant, God told them that in three quick days, they were going somewhere, somewhere they had long been dreaming about. If you personally are in a desert season, remember that God can quickly bring you out of the desert just as he did with the Israelites. Despite the situation, have hope that one day God will say, "Pack your bags; you aren't going to have to wander around in this desert anymore; you are going into your promised land." That promise keeps me plodding along when I find myself in the midst of a desert season.

It isn't spelled out in Scripture, but I imagine if you filled in the blanks, there was some apprehension and a fair amount of fear when Joshua came into camp and said, "Get your supplies ready. Three days from now you will cross the Jordan here to go in and take possession of the land…" (Josh 1:11). This was a people who knew nothing about warfare. All they had done was wander for the past forty years. This was going to be a major change.

When I was in graduate school studying marriage and family therapy, I learned that change, no matter how good or positive, will be resisted. As a leader and counselor, I can tell you that this principle has proven correct in my experiences over the years. Even though the Israelites had been wandering for forty years in the desert, it was the only thing they knew. It was similar to the pattern when they came out of Egypt from slavery; they asked more than once to go back to the "good old days" of Egypt. I imagine there was some serious murmuring in the camp.

People were probably asking a lot of questions: What will it be like? Can we defeat the giants in the land? Remember when we tried this last time? What if we can't make it across the Jordan? What if the water is too deep? What if all our supplies get wet and we don't have any dry clothes to wear? What if we get over there and we get ambushed? At least we can control getting up, wandering around, and setting up camp. Even though this is a terrible place and we have been wandering around in this hot, seemingly endless desert for forty years, at least we know what to expect.

It seems crazy to think that they would even hesitate to move from the desert to the Promised Land. But think about it—the Israelites had known only the desert, even though it wasn't the best existence. They were comfortable with the process: get up and wander around, set up camp, get up, wander around, set up camp—all the while getting nowhere, but at least being comfortable with the routine. Can you relate to being stuck in a routine? I often find myself in routines that keep me from moving forward. Fear can keep us in the same old routine, thereby keeping us from moving on to the destination God has called us to. God often calls us to places that cause us to risk: just read about Abraham, Moses, Noah, Gideon, Jesus, the disciples, and countless others. A quick look at Scripture indicates that in almost all cases when God wants someone to do something big for him, he calls them out of their comfort zone.

Comfort often has its drawbacks. It can keep us in the same dead-end job that is getting us nowhere: get up, go to work, eat dinner, watch television, go to bed, get up, go to work, eat dinner, watch television, go to bed. We know that the dreams we have will never come true staying in this rut, but comfort keeps us there.

Comfort also can keep us in unhealthy relationships. Because conflict is uncomfortable, we often only talk about surface issues and never go deep and address issues that we need to deal with in our relationships. Friendships stay on the surface, marriages stay emotionally disconnected, and families keep secrets. It is more comfortable for us to talk on the surface and to avoid conflict at all cost. This sense of comfort often keeps us from going to the promised land of intimacy.

I can relate. Having been single for thirty-seven years, I had some comfortable routines and ways of doing life and I could regulate how close people got to me; I kept people at a distance when it came to deep relationships. When I did get married to my princess at age thirty-seven, I married a very relational woman who is a master of going deep with people. Put that together: a person who likes to stay on the surface in relationships and one who likes to go deep. As you can imagine, there was some friction. Maybe you are thinking sandpaper friction, but it was more like lighting dynamite! Yet, because of the patience of Candace and her persistence in drilling deep into my heart, I experienced a level of intimacy in a relationship like never before. This moving out of my comfort zone also helped me in my relationships outside my marriage. I could see changes in my leadership and in friendships.

Comfort can also keep us from investing time in others, especially those who may be younger than we are. What if they don't accept me? What will we do together? I am more comfortable just giving some money to the youth fund, singles ministry, or young married group. Fear and comfort can both keep us from running alongside the next generation of runners and passing the baton.

Before we are too hard on the Israelites, let's put our lives into perspective. God often has trouble getting us to move to where he wants to take us because we struggle with the fact that we have to give up control. For many, like myself, control and comfort go together. When I think I am in control, I feel comfortable. When I feel out of control, I feel uncomfortable. That is why we try to control our spouses, our kids, our friends, our activities, our job situations, and our churches. We like to think we are in control. We convince ourselves that comfort is better than a loss of control.

In reality, we never were in control to begin with, but somehow we fooled ourselves into believing that we were. This false sense of control often gets us stuck in the desert, keeping us from moving on into the promised land. It often keeps us from coaching and running alongside the next generation to make a smooth baton pass.

Trying to be in control is something that is born within us. Candace and I have a little three-year-old. For the most part, she is the sweetest girl, but there are those times where she willfully disobeys in order to be in charge. For example, the other day she threw a temper tantrum and was sent to time out. If she would have stayed in time out for three minutes, life would have been good and we would have moved on. But she didn't. Time after time, she would get out of time out and we would have to put her back in. After much longer than three minutes, she still wouldn't obey. After much crying and many temper tantrums, she was starting to calm down, and I said, "You can get out of time out if you tell Daddy you are sorry." She willfully wouldn't do it. So back in time out she went with her crying and screaming. Ten to fifteen minutes later, I sat her on my lap and said, "Honey, all you have to do is say you are sorry and this will all be over. You can get out of time out." Nope, she still wouldn't do it. I was wondering—for those who remember the show Happy Days—whether she was related to the Fonz? She would not say sorry because she wanted to control the situation. Back into time out she went.

Now she was crying and throwing a tantrum so loud that I shut the door of the room she was in. She cried louder. I opened the door and told her, "Honey, all you have to do is say you are sorry and you can get out of time out." She informed me that she said she was sorry when the door was closed! I calmly let her know she needed to say it to my face." And she said, "I only have one sorry!"

Control—we all want it and it starts early. Just to relieve any fears, our daughter isn't still in time out! She finally gave up control and got out. God wants us to give up control and let him lead us. Often he pushes us to risk and get out of our comfort zone in our interaction with others, especially as it relates to passing the baton to the next generation.

How often we see the raging waters of our lives and wonder how we are going to cross them. Or we wonder how we're going to come out alive if the waters get any deeper. When we realize that we were never really in control, but God is, a new perspective comes. The water still is raging, but it doesn't seem as overwhelming. The journey still is scary, but we trust a guide who has crossed it before. It is helpful to remember that in order for God to lead us to the promised land, we have to give up our false sense of control and comfortableness.

I can relate to this giving up control. One day when I was helping lead a trip in Honduras, my group went to the edge of an intense waterfall. Thousands of gallons of water were pouring over and pounding the rocks below. You would get mist sprayed on you from fifty to eighty yards away. A young Honduran teenager at the falls, probably no more than sixteen, was making money by guiding people under the falls. We hired him, not knowing him, and trusted him to get us there. As we started getting closer and closer, the water was pounding off the falls and the mist was drenching us. We had to jump in the river and wade in water about waist to chest high toward the fall. We got to a point where the water was so forceful that we could barely see out in front of us. I will have to be honest here, I was fearful. Okay, I was scared! We had to join hands in a line to be able to go farther. We couldn't see the guide, but we just followed the person whose hand we had grasped. I wondered what we had gotten ourselves into; we were at the mercy of a teenage entrepreneur guide.

Control was completely out of our hands, and it was a scary and uncomfortable place to be. I wondered if this was it, if we would be lost in the falls? Then it became even more intense. The guide led us to an area about three feet wide behind the falls where the water pressure was so forceful that it was hard to breathe. I was feeling claustrophobic and pushed my way to the front to be able to breathe. Forget servant leadership, I was trying to live! Back in there was a tiny cave just large enough for two people to fit into and explore. Then I looked around and the guide was gone. I thought to myself, if he doesn't come back, how are we going to get out of here? It was a total feeling of loss of all control and was way out of my comfort zone. He did eventually come back and we made it out alive. It remains one of those, after the fact, "that was awesome," once-in-a-lifetime experiences, but if we hadn't pushed through, it would have never happened. It was amazing and one of the highlights in my outdoor adventures. If I had known all the hazards or the risk factors in advance, I may have never gone and experienced one of the most exhilarating adventures of my life.

I wonder how many incredible, exhilarating adventures we miss because of our desire to be comfortable. We may completely pass on some exciting, life-changing adventures that God has lined up with members of a younger generation because we are too comfortable running the race alone or only running with those we have run together with for years. Where is God asking you to take a risk? What areas in your life hold you back from running the race at full speed because of control or comfort issues? Is your wandering causing you to miss the promised land God is calling you to?

Application Questions

1. Do you agree that familiarity with spiritual things may keep us from doing great things for God?

2. Do you have an example of how that happened in your life or an example of how God called you to get out of your "comfort zone" to make a difference in someone else's life?

3. Have you ever struggled to give up control of some aspect of your life? In what areas are you reluctant to give God control?

4. Do you believe God is calling you to take more risks in some areas of your life?

5. If so, what first step could you take in response to him?

Chapter Four

Raising Up a Generation Who GETS IT

How do we pass the baton? How do we keep from becoming another page in the history books of a generation that didn't hand the baton off well?

In my travels across North America, I continue to have conversations with students who have grown up in the church yet are confused about their faith. While working with a group during a large student conference, I helped find a worship band that could play a few songs during the main service after the primary worship leader had to leave early. One option was a high school student worship band that played regularly at a large church they attended and came with high recommendations. The conference ended up letting this band play and they seemed to do a great job. Later they were given an even bigger role. Sometime later, I happened to look at one of the primary band member's social website and was amazed. The F-bombs were flying, God stuff was zero, and his lifestyle had taken a turn that looked more like it could be a part of the movie *Hangover* rather than *The Passion of the Christ*. What happened? Here was a young man who had been in church for years, had parents who were Christ followers, was in leadership in his church, and even had his gifts and talents affirmed on a national level outside the church. What happened in the spiritual formation process? Where was the baton dropped?[1]

It isn't happening just among those who are in high school and college. There are numerous individuals in their twenties, thirties, and forties who have had a lot of interaction with the church in their younger years and have left the faith. As reported earlier, research indicates that a majority of twentysomethings—61% of today's young adults—had been churched at one point during their teen years but

---

1. My prayer and hope is that he comes back to the faith as he grows. He has incredible leadership ability.

are now spiritually disengaged (i.e., not actively attending church, reading the Bible, or praying). Only 20% have maintained a level of spiritual activity consistent with their high school experiences.[2] In my own experience, I have interacted with many who grew up in the church but now find it irrelevant to their lives.

Take my friend Joe, who's now in his forties. He grew up in the church but has lived for years outside of the church community, living a life of promiscuity and living in the party scene. A great guy, but the baton of faith wasn't handed off.

Or look at Tom,[3] a student who was involved in our youth ministry. He came to almost everything that went on in our ministry, and was even a regular on mission trips. He was involved in numerous hours of spiritual discussions yet is reported to live a life that would be far different from what Scripture teaches to be Christ-centered.

What is happening? Why is research showing that we as a church aren't making smooth hand offs? Why are the majority of individual believers not handing the baton off well? Is it because many churches have become more of a country club than a hospital? Is it because we as individuals have to work hard to impress when we are with "spiritual" people rather than be real? Is the Christianity we teach different from the Christianity we live? Is it that we compartmentalize and separate our daily life from our spiritual life? Are we more concerned about the right behavior than making sure people have a true relationship with Jesus? We have to honestly ask the question when it comes to passing the baton, are we really any different from Joshua and his generation in the book of Judges? Where are we failing in the spiritual formation and discipling of the younger generations?

There seem to be some myths in the church about spiritual formation and discipleship. To make sure we are on the same page, I

2. Barna Group, "Most Twentysomethings Put Christianity on the Shelf Following Spiritually Active Teen Years" (Barna.org, September 11, 2006), http://www.barna.org/barna-update/article/16-teensnext-gen/147-most-twentysomethings-put-christianity-on-the-shelf-following-spiritually-active-teen-years?q=teens+church.

3. The student's name has been changed.

will refer to discipleship and spiritual formation interchangeably for the remainder of this book. I believe there are five myths that have been detrimental in the passing of the baton. Unless we recognize these myths, we run the high risk of continuing, as churches and as individuals, to drop the baton of faith as we try to pass it.

MYTH 1: PEOPLE BECOME DISCIPLES BY ATTENDING A LOCAL CHURCH.

The belief that individuals become mature disciples of Christ by just attending a service on a weekend at a local church keeps many churches with immature believers. The writer of Hebrews weighs in on this:

> We have much to say about this, but it is hard to explain because you are slow to learn. In fact, though by this time you ought to be teachers, you need someone to teach you the elementary truths of God's word all over again. You need milk, not solid food! Anyone who lives on milk, being still an infant, is not acquainted with the teaching about righteousness. (Heb 5:11–13)

If we think that people grow into mature believers from a Sunday morning or a Saturday night message only, we are deceiving ourselves. Don't get me wrong, attending corporate worship is very important to our spiritual growth (Heb 10:25), but just attending a corporate worship service doesn't necessarily make disciples.

This hit home for me in a mind numbing way when I talked to a couple of students who had been under my ministry for about five years and who had probably heard more than two hundred of my messages. One day at an ice cream shop, I asked "What do you remember from all the lessons you heard at…" and I named the program. "What do you remember?" What I was really asking them was which messages made a difference in their lives. Most of the messages I had worked hard on to make them relevant, to give application, and to help make a difference in their walk with Jesus. Their reply was sobering, yet also awakening. They remembered two or three stand–alone messages and two or three series. Think about that, maybe fifteen messages at most out of more than two hundred—not even 10%.

I have done a similar experiment in a university class setting with students and found that those who grew up in the church remember very few of the messages taught from the platform. I am not suggesting our messages don't have an impact and that we shouldn't devote quality time and effort in preparing and giving them. But I am suggesting that those of us in church leadership need to reexamine our method for disciple making. If we are expecting our church community to become strong disciples of Christ from only our Sunday morning message, we may be no different in our thinking than the type of people who would be convinced to buy swamp land in the desert.

Maybe the way we worship as a church needs to be reexamined. I was sitting in a church service recently, listening to a message in a relevant church with good communicators. I wondered whether the lecture-type sermon that the majority of our churches are centered around, especially in the United States, is the best way to help people become disciples of Christ. Is there a better and more creative way to help people internalize and live out the gospel? How do we help the message to permeate their being so that Christ truly becomes a part of their core? Sure, many of today's churches have high-tech video and some have drama, as my local church does, but the lecture-style message is still what many consider the main component. Are there other creative ways to help pass the baton and aid spiritual forma-tion? In our interactive society, are there creative ways to get people involved in living out the message? If we are depending on Sunday morning lecture-style only to pass the baton, we are investing in low return stock.

MYTH 2: TIME BRINGS SPIRITUAL MATURITY.

If this myth were true, church issues and fights among those in church communities would always happen with children rather than adults. If you have been in a local church for any time, you have probably had the unfortunate experience of seeing the nasty side of church politics.

In many cases, some of those who can be the most disruptive and nastiest are those who have been a part of that local church the longest. I could tell you some horror stories from watching my parents (retired pastors) in their pastoral ministry. I have seen individuals get very rude—even downright mean. It is by the grace of God and the faithfulness of my parents that I am even a part of the church. By the way some people acted, you would wonder if they even knew who Jesus was, let alone whether they had a relationship with him. In nine out of the ten cases, most were longtime church members.

Let's face it, time alone doesn't bring spiritual maturity. I have known many teenagers who were much more mature in their faith than fifty- and sixty-year-olds who had been going to a local church all their lives. Time, as a believer and in a local church, doesn't bring about spiritual maturity. Interacting with other believers in a corporate worship experience is a crucial part of becoming spiritually mature, but just entering a church building every week for years doesn't bring about spiritual maturity. If this myth were true and those who attended church became mature by just being there, than it wouldn't take one hundred persons in the average evangelical church in America to influence an average of 1.67 persons to Christ each year—less than two persons coming to Christ per one hundred church members a year![4]

MYTH 3: ONE SHOULD INVEST MORE TIME IN THE MASSES THAN IN THE FEW.

Some leaders would admit this; others would deny it; but many leaders in our churches are more concerned about numbers than they are about changing people. More numbers mean more people, which mean more hear about Jesus. This is true; yet if all leaders were honest, sometimes our motives are more about how successful we look than about the actual life change that happens. The more people we have in our churches, the better we are doing, right? Not exactly. There are

---

4. T-Net International, "The White Paper: A Comprehensive Guide to T-NET," tnetwork.com, accessed March 26, 2012, http://www.tnetwork.com/WhitePaper.htm.

many churches and programs that have and are still attracting crowds but are not healthy places to be. Growth and health don't always go together. On the other hand, health and growth always go together. In other words, a growing place doesn't always mean a healthy place, but a healthy place will always foster growth. The church growth movement has been good in helping us be concerned about growth, but some may have misinterpreted it to mean we should be more concerned about numbers than spiritual formation.

Jesus had a short time in ministry—three years or so. He knew in advance this was all the time he would have. Wouldn't it be nice to know how much time you have? Jesus could draw a crowd, but where did you find him focusing most of his time? Instead of having the five thousand he fed and taught (really more like fifteen to twenty thousand when women and children are included) every weekend, he focused on the Twelve. He then poured himself even more intensely into three of the Twelve. Why? Did Jesus know something we didn't? Of course, he is God!

He knew that doing life with a few in community would have a greater impact than spending his weekends with the thousands. Because of his investment in the Twelve, I am writing this book, and because of his investment in the Twelve, you are reading it. Eleven of those men took what Jesus taught them and spread that message around the world so we could have new life in Christ. Yet if we take a look at our churches and their leaders, what are they most concerned about? Having more people at their weekend service or making sure that lives are being changed? I often find that churches and church leaders put a lot of pressure on the pastoral staff they oversee to produce numbers, but very little time is spent discussing what strategy is in place to have a life-changing impact on those who are currently there and those who will come. "Build it and they will come," but what happens when they come?

Please hear me: I am not proposing that we shouldn't focus on numbers and growth. There is a whole book of the Bible titled Numbers. Numbers are important because they represent people. What I am proposing is that we focus on church health and how we pass the baton rather than how many people we have at a service. If we focus on having healthy churches, they will grow. Considering Jesus had twelve and their influence has reached countless millions, Jesus' primary focus was to pour into a few, knowing that multiplication is more impacting than addition. We need to take notice.

MYTH 4: AN INTENTIONAL DISCIPLESHIP PLAN IS NOT NECESSARY TO PRODUCE SPIRITUAL GROWTH.

Believing that spiritual growth will just happen is almost as absurd as believing that simply hanging out on a college campus will earn one a PhD. I wish my PhD had come that easily! As church leaders, we can't just hope it happens. We can't just hope that the spiritual babies God gives us become mature without having a plan to help them get there. Maybe that is why God doesn't give spiritual babies to a lot of churches. They don't know how to take care of them.

Before my wife and I had our first child, we read all kinds of material to figure out what to do during the pregnancy and how to care for our future newborn. When our baby was born, we would have been thrown in jail if we had laid her on the couch unattended and gone on about our daily lives, telling people about our newborn but never caring for her and addressing her needs. This would have resulted in our baby's death. Why? Because it was our responsibility to help nurture this baby and we would have failed to do so. Yet most of our churches rejoice when a newborn in the faith is added. They talk about it with others and use it when reporting their numbers; and many genuinely rejoice, as we should. But many of those newborns just lie on the couch, waiting for us to help them learn how to grow. In reality, most churches don't have an intentional plan to nurture those young believers. This, if we really want to be real, is no better than bringing a physical newborn into the world and neglecting it.

I remember when our first child was a newborn; she took a lot of energy and time, and oh how I missed sleep. Despite the many late nights, the time invested was worth every minute. Candace and I want to do all we can to help her develop and grow. Discipleship is work, and caring for new believers takes time and often is messy. But aren't spiritual babies as important as physical babies, and shouldn't we be just as intentional with them?

MYTH 5: THE SPIRITUAL FORMATION PROCESS IS THE SOLE RESPONSIBILITY OF CHURCH LEADERSHIP.

Spiritual formation is a responsibility of church leadership, but it is also the responsibility of all individual believers to be involved in the spiritual formation of others. We have a responsibility to help those who are younger then we are to grow and mature in the faith. It is not something left solely for those who hold the title of pastor; it is the responsibility of all believers to be a part of an intentional lifelong strategy to help pass the baton of faith.

Think about this, most churches have one staff member per 150 people. Realistically, can one person be investing and pouring into 150 individual people? Can that one staff member spend time and really get to know and nurture 150 people in life? Of course not. If you don't believe me, try it. The spiritual formation of others, or passing the baton, is part of each believer's responsibility. Jesus, in the Great Commission, gives us all this important responsibility. Whether you have been a believer for fifty years or for one year, whether you are eighty or fourteen, it is your responsibility as Christ-followers to pour into others and help them mature in the faith.

You may think you aren't mature enough to be a part of the spiritual formation process; you feel you haven't arrived. Let's face it: this spiritual journey is a constant journey in which we will never arrive until we are face-to-face with Jesus. If we waited to pour into someone else until we "have arrived," no one could ever pour into anyone else. If we have a relationship with Jesus and want to grow in our faith, it is our responsibility to pour into others, to pass the baton of faith. And the incredible benefit is that often through this process we grow to be more of who God desires us to be.

I propose we need a paradigm shift in discipleship. We need to revisit how most of us have defined and think about passing the baton. Spiritual formation is more than curriculum or a Sunday school class. I believe strongly in spiritual formation curriculum. (I helped write a four-level series for teenagers called the Ultimate Adventure and invested numerous hours in that project.[5]) Don't misunderstand me, I believe curriculum is needed in the discipleship process, but curriculum without life on life isn't very effective. We can have the best material in the world, but if we aren't godly examples, being guided by Scripture and intentionally investing time in the younger generations, we are producing individuals who have head knowledge but know nothing about it from the heart.

It reminds me of a story I heard years ago about a student who knew dozens of Bible verses. He was always winning the Bible memory quizzes and knew all the information. Yet when there were some things stolen at the church, guess who it was? Yep, Mr. Bible Verse. He had all the head knowledge but not the heart knowledge. It seems a lot of our ministries are producing individuals who have a lot of head knowledge and even do the right thing on Sundays, but don't have it embedded in their hearts. Too often this scenario plays out when a student goes off to college and is challenged in their faith: they bail on it quickly. Could it be because they only have it in their intellect and not in their heart? It can happen to adults too. When believers (not necessarily new believers) are challenged by friends at work or in another social setting, they may quickly walk the other way or adapt to the behavior of the group if they haven't been grounded in their faith.

It reminds me of how I used to study in many of my classes in college. I made great grades; I graduated undergrad with a 4.0. Yep, summa cum laude, but I don't say that in a bragging way because many students who had a 2.0 probably know more than I do about some of those subjects. In most cases, I would memorize for the test and get a good grade on the test. Yet if you asked me two days later to share some facts about that material, I would have trouble sharing it with you. I only did what was necessary to get the grade by doing the right things, having the right behavior, getting the kudos from

---

5. You can find the Ultimate Adventure series at www.chogy.org under Resources or by contacting Warner Press and asking for the Ultimate Adventure series (800-741-7721 or www.warnerpress.org).

the professors, but never internalizing the majority of the material. Unfortunately, I am convinced that many in our churches are living the same way—going to church, saying the right things to the pastor, giving funds to the church, being recognized as leaders but not having a heart-transforming experience such that Christ becomes the center of everything.

Whether it is the education system we have created or the church world we have created, head knowledge by itself is not going to help the younger generations live their faith in a world that is often hostile to their faith. So what do we do? How do we help people go deeper than just head knowledge? How do we pass the baton? What is true discipleship? If we analyze Scripture there are numerous examples of passing the baton of faith.

The most obvious of course is Jesus. He invested in a small group of twelve to do life with and even a smaller group of three to go even deeper. If you put this in perspective, it is an interesting method. Jesus knew that life-on-life, intentional investment of time and being a godly example in a small setting, was what truly makes a difference. Jesus realized that he could impress from a distance, but he could really have an impact up close.[6]

There are numerous examples of others who invested in a few younger individuals. Paul and Timothy, Naomi and Ruth, Moses and Joshua, and more. If you study what happened in these relationships, spiritual formation boils down to a simple process:

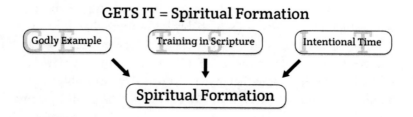

GETS IT = Spiritual Formation

Godly Example   Training in Scripture   Intentional Time

Spiritual Formation

---

6. Howard Hendricks, *Teaching to Change Lives* (Sisters, OR: Multnomah Publishers, 1987), 89.

This is a simple but life-changing equation. If we would live as godly examples, training the younger generations to be guided by Scripture and intentionally investing time in their lives, the baton of faith would be passed off smoothly.

If you look back almost three thousand years ago to the book of Judges, this is why Joshua and the leaders failed. They failed to be godly examples. They failed to help the younger generation hear God's word. They failed to intentionally invest time. They failed to pass the baton. Is that going to be our story? *If we don't invest life on life in the younger generations, we are in danger of losing the church.* The last few generations, especially those born since 1965, seem confused about their faith, and we in the church have to shoulder some of the blame. Somewhere, somehow, we have missed it. We often agonize over the behavior and belief systems of the upcoming generations under us, but we need to understand something. For many of us, these are our children, our grandchildren, our brothers and sisters, and we have a responsibility for them.

Some would say we are only one generation away from the extinction of Christianity. Is the description of the North American church as one mile wide and one inch deep correct? Have we been so focused on church growth that we neglect to see the demise of church health? Are we good at attracting crowds but not so good at investing in them?

What would happen if we intentionally invested time, were godly examples, were guided by Scripture, and poured ourselves into the younger generations to help them discover what it means to have an incredible, passionate relationship with the one and only God of the universe? What would happen if we started investing in one or two individuals who are younger than we are? What would happen if we followed in the footsteps of Jesus, Paul, and Naomi? What would happen if we quit raising up individuals in our churches who only have head knowledge but instead raised up people who have passionate heart knowledge and incorporate Jesus into daily actions?

We aren't going to pass the faith on because we have big buildings, great youth centers, big events, and silver-tongued communicators.

Those can be important components, but they are a means and not an end. If we would stop spending so much time deciding on what color the carpet should be, what program we are going to have, what worship style we are going to use, or how we are going to market the church to attract more people, and instead spent the same amount of time and effort investing life on life in someone younger than we are, the church would be a different place. Parents, if we spent as much time in planning for our kids' spiritual formation as we do researching our new car or electronic purchase or spent as much time investing in them as we do watching television during the week, the spiritual landscape of our churches and our communities would change.

GETS IT = Spiritual Formation

Godly Example   Training in Scripture   Intentional Time

Spiritual Formation

Yes, it seems simple. You are right, it's not rocket science. It's not even a program. If you bought this book to learn a complex strategy for spiritual formation, I'm sorry to disappoint you; true biblical spiritual formation is a simple process. I think we often try to complicate things in our Christian world. Jesus modeled disciple-ship simply as intentionally investing time in his disciples and being a godly example for them to observe. What about you? Have you complicated things when it comes to spiritual formation? Have you relied on and left it up to pastors or the church leaders around you to be the disciples for your children and the younger generations that you encounter? The book of Judges would have had a different ending if everyone would have purposely realized they had a baton to hand off. We all have a baton. What are you going to do with it?

Application Questions

1. Barna Research Group reports that only one-fifth of Christians in their twenties maintain the level of spiritual activity they had in high school. What factors might account for this weakening discipleship?

2. Review the five myths of discipleship mentioned in the chapter. Do you agree with them? Why or why not?

3. Do you think American churches have done a good job of instilling heart knowledge of Christ, as well as head knowledge? What about your local congregation?

4. Some would say that the spirituality of a typical North American church is "a mile wide and an inch deep." Do you agree? Why or why not?

5. How can you live out the GETS IT principle of spiritual formation (Godly Example + Training in Scripture + Intentional Time)? What specific steps can you take to begin practicing it?

Chapter Five

Where Are the Runners Who Finish Strong?

GODLY EXAMPLES

Anyone who has spent any time around professed Christians can probably bring to mind someone who claimed to be a believer in Christ but who then did something that was far from what Christ would have done or how he commanded us to live. Some acts are so heinous we can't even bear to think of them. From national and international leaders to small-town Christian leaders, there have been devastating moral failures that have affected not only the victims but often hundreds and sometimes thousands of individuals due to the ripple effect. Some might wonder, Where have all the godly examples gone?

Your parents may have professed to be followers of Christ but your home life was more like a battle zone than a place where the Prince of Peace was in control. Or other people that you trusted as spiritual leaders become as trustworthy as Al Capone. What happens when you are constantly exposed to these conflicting messages or situations? You often become skeptical, cynical, or antagonistic, losing all hope that there is a perfect Savior who died and loves you. I speak from experience, as I was affected by a mentor who lived a double life.

When I was in high school, I had the privilege of having a youth pastor who had a dynamic and charismatic personality. He was one of those guys you wanted to hang around. He was sharp, a great communicator, and good with people. He invested in me, taught me, challenged me, and spent time with me. He mentored me in how to share the love of Jesus with others.

On some Saturday mornings, we would go to apartment complexes, knock on doors, and ask individuals if they had any children living with them. If they did, we would ask them if their children could come to children's church (a special program for kids at our local church) the next day if they didn't have a home church. I know, it sounds weird today to make cold calls on people, but twenty-plus years ago it worked in some places. So on Sundays I would go back with a school bus (they didn't let me drive, even though that would have been fun as a sixteen-year-old) and I would help pick up the kids for children's church. I really admired this youth leader. He was fun, creative, incredibly talented, gifted in dealing with people and a great teacher. I wanted to be like him.

In my senior year of high school, my world was turned upside down. This youth pastor, who was married and had two young children, had an affair with another one of our married volunteer youth leaders. I was devastated. Was all the stuff he had taught me about Christ really true? I started to doubt everything. As I went into my freshman year of college, I was angry at my youth leader, God, and the church. I didn't want anything to do with any of it. I felt that no one outside of my family could be trusted.

During my freshman year of college, I would schedule myself to work on Sundays so I wouldn't feel guilty for not going to church services. I was running from God and wanted nothing to do with organized religion. My behavior was all about me. I lived on the fence, as they say, not really wanting to jump totally away from God and other believers, but not sure I wanted what it all entailed. I would have probably bailed on God and the church and would currently be living quite a different lifestyle if my parents hadn't lived as true godly examples and built a foundation that led me to realize how life with Christ should be, and could be, lived. If it hadn't been for their examples, I would have been lost to the faith. After a year or two of struggling with all that had happened, God finally got through to me and helped me understand one of the most important lessons I have ever learned and one that sustains me today: people will fail you, but God never will.

So what does all this mean for those of us who really want to make a difference but have had people who said one thing and lived another? How do we make sure we don't have similar stories? What about the thousands of people out there who are yearning for someone who really lives a life after Christ, someone who truly walks the walk instead of just talking the talk. The majority of individuals don't have many godly examples they can turn to and often our exposure to them is the only light they see. We have to take to heart Jesus' words in Matthew 5, "You are the salt of the earth and light of the world." We have a responsibility to be Christ-centered leaders who passionately love and obey God, sacrificially serve others, intentionally share Christ, and experience Christian community. We need to realize that it is God's goal to transform the world through his love and he uses us to do that. We have to recognize that not only do our lifestyles affect us, but they have powerful effects on those around us, especially those who are younger than we are. They are depending on us.

Being a Christ-follower is more than just attending a local church. It is more than putting some of our resources in an offering plate or box, more than doing a few projects where we help the down-and-outers, and more than even doing our environmental duty to help save the planet. The Christian walk is a lifestyle of love, and it looks different from that of those who don't know Christ—not in a way that says I am better than you or look at me for what I do or don't do. It is a lifestyle that wants to see how close we can get to walking in the footsteps of Jesus because of our love for him and for others due to the heart change that only he can bring.

In the Jewish culture, the brightest young men would study under a particular rabbi. There was a saying for those who were chosen as the top students to shadow a rabbi: "Cover yourself with the dust of your rabbi's feet." In other words, may you get so close to your teacher while following him that when he walks the dusty streets, the dust from his steps covers you.[1] Instead, it seems that many of

---

1. Rob Bell, *Velvet Elvis: Repainting the Christian Faith* (Grand Rapids, MI: Zondervan, 2005), 130.

us in our Christian communities often ask the question, some of us consciously, but most of us subconsciously, How close can I get to the line? Or to phrase it another way, How can I behave and be like everyone else around me and still be a Christ-follower?

It is interesting that Scripture actually talks about the Christian life as being one that really doesn't fit in. Jesus says in Matthew 5:11–12, " Blessed are you when people insult you, persecute you and falsely say all kinds of evil against you because of me. Rejoice and be glad, because great is your reward in heaven, for in the same way they persecuted the prophets who were before you."

Maybe we are asking the wrong question. Perhaps the question should be, How close can I get to Jesus? When we ask that question, a lot of what we thought was important to us becomes unimportant. We find that many of the items on our list of things okay to be involved in aren't really necessary. We experience a change of heart.

I'm not saying that we should alienate ourselves from society, but people should notice a difference in us. Matthew 5:14 says, "You are the light of the world. A city on a hill cannot be hidden." The book of Acts records stories of Christ-followers living in such a way that there was a noticeable difference in how they did life, such a difference that the kingdom of God grew at an astonishing rate.

Our enemy, Satan, is very sly. Often when we make heart changes that result in behavioral changes, our changes are for the right reasons. Yet if we aren't careful, the enemy can take those changes and over time turn them into a legalistic set of dos and don'ts. What takes place is that we start to look down on those who don't do as we do. It reminds me of the Dr. Seuss story of the star-bellied sneetches and the plain-bellied sneetches. In this children's story, the sneetches with stars on their bellies were accepted, but those who did not have stars on their bellies were ostracized.[2] Sometimes we are like that in the church; those who do or don't do certain behaviors are in, and those who do or don't do certain things are looked down upon. What began

---

2. Geisel Theodor Seuss, *The Sneetches, and Other Stories* (New York: Random House, 1961).

as behaviors with good motives can end up having a negative effect on our faith walk later. Trust me, I know.

I trusted Christ early in my life and grew up in a pastor's home. Many of our activities centered around the church and spiritual things. I really wanted to please God, yet at the same time, especially as I became an older teenager, I wanted to please myself. I tried to live a life for Jesus while also trying to stay as close as possible to the line of how everyone around me was behaving.

After my negative experience with my youth pastor and the double life he lived, and even after God taught me the lesson that people will fail us but God never will, I still struggled throughout my college years with my faith walk. After college I took a role in a church as a youth pastor. I was determined that if I was going to be in that role, I was going to be in it all the way. I had experienced what could happen if someone didn't live what they taught. I wanted to be different. I wanted to live as a totally devoted follower of Jesus. So I totally committed my heart and life to God to be all that he wanted me to be. I wanted to be so close to Jesus and move as far away as I could from the line of mediocrity. I gave up things in my life that I thought were hindering my relationship with God and started doing "the right things"(e.g., Scripture reading, praying, fasting). At that time, my spiritual behaviors were for the right reasons. I gave up things in my life, such as certain types of music and other media that were having an ungodly effect on me or had anything associated with them that would have been questionable. My motives were right at that time and I grew in my walk with Jesus.

Yet, as the enemy is so sly, years later he took what were heartfelt motives in the beginning and turned them into a legalistic checklist of dos and don'ts. A decade later I was doing some of the same things, not out of a heart for God, but because I had always done them, and if I have to be honest, many times because I was applauded and lifted up as this great person of discipline. In reality, my relationship with God had become more of a checklist than a relationship. This caused me to look at others doing or not doing the same things as I was doing as being "less than." Were those things I did wrong? Of course not! They were spiritual disciplines and important to my growth in Christ. Unfortunately, my motivations for doing them had gotten misplaced in the process. Just as in Old Testament days, offering sacrifices without a heart for God wasn't God's plan. First Samuel 15:22 says, "Does the LORD delight in burnt offerings and sacrifices as much as in obeying the LORD? To obey is better than sacrifice, and to heed is better than the fat of rams."

Making Christianity about a list of dos and don'ts and removing the heart and love of why we serve God, is one reason there are many individuals in our churches who are now cranky and legalistic. I believe that many of these started out with great intentions but have lost the heart behind why they do what they do. That is why we must constantly examine our motives for our actions. It is such a slippery slope to go either way, to the conforming side or to the legalistic side. We have to constantly search our heart and see if it matches God's heart. Why do we do what we do? Is it because of a checklist or because we think God will love us more when we do certain things? On the other hand, do we avoid behaviors because we don't want to stand out or be radical for Jesus? Are we more concerned about our selfish desires or wanting to have our freedom than we are about the heart of God? Or have we grown up around legalistic people and do everything we can to not be like that, often doing behaviors because of our past issues and not because we have been directed by God? The defining question we should be asking about everything we do is, What would God want me to do?

Not asking this question may be what happened to Christian leaders in the last thirty years who have had moral failures. I won't mention names, but I am sure that some will come to mind. I think it would be safe to say that the majority of those leaders, if not all, started out doing the right things, following and pointing people to Christ. Yet over time something happened, little by little, closer and closer to the line the enemy pulled them, busier and busier they became, and an unexamined life led to a big fall. I could fill pages and pages of this chapter about deacons, elders, pastors, and religious leaders who have done some terrible things to others. Unfortunately,

I have personally known more people than I care to know who fall in this category.

The reality is that people aren't perfect and people will fail. Yet, some of these life-changing failures could have been avoided. Often as believers, we accept Christ and stay at that point. Many of us spend more time researching which car we are going to buy than we do on God's word to us in Scripture. We often make the first step but stay there. Paul talked about this in 1 Corinthians 3:1–2, "Brothers, I could not address you as spiritual but as worldly—mere infants in Christ. I gave you milk, not solid food, for you were not yet ready for it. Indeed, you are still not ready."

Sometime back, I was doing some study in the book of Romans and was pouring over the Romans 12:2 passage, which reads, "Do not conform any longer to the pattern of this world, but be transformed by the renewing of your mind. Then you will be able to test and approve what God's will is—his good, pleasing and perfect will." As I think about the current Christian community, I wonder if there is really a difference in our behavior? We often drink the same drinks, smoke the same substances, watch the same movies, say the same off-color words, wear the same revealing clothes, talk and gossip about people (often behind the guise of prayer concern), hold the same grudges, look down on the have-nots, hold on to our money like it is ours and not God's, and struggle to even give him 10%. Is there really any difference between someone who has a relationship with Christ and someone who doesn't? Some would say the difference is that we love people. Yet, if I am honest, I have often seen those without a relationship with Christ love people as well as and sometimes better than some who claim to have a relationship with Christ.

I am not saying we should make Christianity about all these dos and don'ts in a legalistic way. What sets Christianity apart from every other religion is its core. At Christianity's core is an active grace in our relationships with God and others. Yet, at the same time Scripture is clear that followers of Jesus Christ are called to live their lives on a higher standard (for example, Rom 12:2; 2 Cor 5:20–21; Gal 5:19–26; 1 Peter 1:14–16). Our love for God and for others, inspired by his love, should spur us on to live a life that displays grace and love. The younger generation yearns to see leaders who are honestly and consistently asking themselves, What would God want me to do?

A quote attributed to Socrates says, "An unexamined life isn't worth living." We must constantly examine where we are in our relationship with Christ, making sure we are hearing the voice of God and obeying that voice. We need to make sure we are living out of a heart of love for God and others, not out of what we think benefits us or what we believe is our right. Let God be the one to talk to you, not some book, popular spiritual leader, magazine, or rating system, not even those you hang around. Take your Bible out and a journal and examine your life. We should always be asking ourselves, What would God want me to do?

I challenge you to ask the question of what it really looks like to be holy or set apart for God (1 Peter 1:15–16)? What responsibility do I have to those who are around me, especially those younger than I or those younger in the faith than I am? Are there things that are permissible but probably not beneficial? Spend a little time in 1 Corinthians, chapters six and eight, and let God speak to your heart.

If we look back at the last thirty years, there have been numerous leaders, or "heroes of the faith," who have made devastating immoral decisions that deeply affected those they led. What if in the next thirty years, the younger generations could write about a period when there were numerous Christ-centered leaders who lived out their faith as godly examples, trained others in Scripture, and intentionally invested time in the younger generation? What if we finished strong? What if there was a future generation who really GETS IT? What if?

Application Questions

1. Consider these two questions: "How closely can I imitate the rest of society and still be a Christian?" and, "How close can I get to Jesus?" Which of these more often guides your behavior?

2. Has a spiritual mentor or exemplary Christian ever let you down in an incredible way? How did you feel and react?

3. How should Christians behave differently from those who don't know Christ? How can we keep Christianity from being merely a list of legalistic behaviors?

4. "Do not conform any longer to the pattern of this world, but be transformed by the renewing of your mind. Then you will be able to test and approve what God's will is—his good, pleasing and perfect will" (Rom 12:2 NIV). What do you think this scripture means for you today?

5. How do you think someone can be a godly example for others? Who has been a godly example in your life? What were some of that person's characteristics?

Chapter Six

Following the Course Map

TRAINING IN SCRIPTURE

Lost! It wasn't the first time and I am sure it won't be the last. There we were in the middle of nowhere on a desert highway with van loads of students. Lost. The students were road-weary and had van fever (a variation of cabin fever) from being cooped up in the van so long. Some were making those infamous sounds as can only be heard in a van full of teenagers; others were trying to carry on a wrestling match over the seats. But everyone was a little stir-crazy, maybe an effect of the fumes that are emitted out of a van full of teenagers loaded with a lot of guys! We were lost, surrounded by chaos, and not sure of our next move.

Most of us have probably been lost at some point in our lives. It can be a scary feeling not knowing where to go or what direction to move in. In our situation, we had a map and were able to get back on course. Today, thank goodness, most of us have a GPS or a tracking system on our phones that helps us know where we are headed. There is even a little dot that tells us where we currently are. If we see that we are off course, we can make a few turns and head back in the direction that we need to go.

Maps and navigation systems are helpful and often essential in helping us get where we need to go. Yet I am sure most of us have experienced a ride or two where the driver, or maybe even you, has tried to get somewhere without looking at the map and has gotten way off course. It depends on the person, but sometimes we drive quite a ways off course before we stop to look at the map or ask directions, often getting even farther away from our destination.

Putting that into the context for life, God's word to us in Scripture is our road map for running this journey called life. So many times we try to run with little or no guidance from Scripture. This is a key component of living a life for Jesus and a key component in helping younger generations understand the direction God wants them to go. That is why one of the necessary components of spiritual formation is **training in Scripture**. When people aren't trained in Scripture, they tend to base their faith on a person or someone else's beliefs rather than discovering who God is for themselves. I have seen more than one college student shaken in their faith when challenged in a university setting because their faith map wasn't based on Scripture but only on what their parents or youth pastor had told them. And now that those influences weren't around, they were lost as to which direction to go.

This is why the key component of training individuals to search, explore, and be guided by Scripture is so essential in handing off the baton of faith smoothly. Being a godly example is vital, and investing time in others is critical; but let's face it, there will be a day when we won't be here on this earth to model or invest time anymore. If we haven't helped those we are investing in understand how to read and be guided by life's roadmap (the Bible), then when other voices or pressures come, it is hard to stay on course.

I think we are often hesitant to make training in Scripture a part of the spiritual formation process. There are some key factors that often hinder us. One, we ourselves may not have a consistent plan to refer back to the roadmap ourselves. I have a friend who is a farmer. I love to talk to him about the crops and the planting and the harvesting. Farmers consistently plant crops in the spring and harvest in the fall. It is a discipline they practice, and when the weather isn't cooperative, they persist and follow through. If they didn't plant, they wouldn't reap a harvest. The same can be said of us; if we aren't giving God a chance to speak into our lives through Scripture, how can we expect to hear from him? How can we train someone else if we ourselves aren't doing it?

The basic remedy for this obstacle is to start incorporating Scripture into our daily routine. There are numerous helps and Bible tools out there. A great free download for smart phones with numerous translations and Bible reading plans can be found at www.youversion. com. Great tools to study and delve into Scripture are available at www.biblegateway.com and www.crosswalk.com. Additional tools for studying Scripture can also be found at www.inword.org, www. navigators.org, and www.navpress.com. There are numerous devotional books and easy-to-read translations; and specialty Bibles can be found at most local Christian bookstores.

If you have never really delved into Scripture or find it cumbersome or hard to understand, ask someone in your spiritual community you respect to coach you and help you get started; they can also suggest some useful resources. The key is to make it a priority. I don't want to sound like this has always been an easy process for me. There have been times I have been disciplined in reading daily Scripture; at other times, I've drifted with an on-and-off pattern. What I have found helpful is to have a specific plan, which is one reason that I love the youversion.com download for my phone. It has specific plans you can choose that take you right to that passage each day. Having Scripture as a daily part of our lives is a major part of the **GETS IT** process in passing the baton.

Another reason we may shy away from helping train others in Scripture is that we feel that it is the pastor's job or the job of someone on our church staff on Sunday. But if we make Sunday morning's message the key component in spiritual formation, we are missing the boat. If this were the case, then the millions who attend church weekly would be making an incredible impact around them. I am not saying there aren't pockets of impact happening, but I would argue that the majority of those who are making a difference don't rely only on a Sunday morning message for their spiritual development.

Something else that may keep us from training others in Scripture is that we ourselves don't feel very comfortable with the Bible and may not know how to find or answer all the questions that we may be asked about in Scripture. Let's be honest, there are some things that seem to be mysteries, and other things aren't specifically mentioned in Scripture. Yet Scripture overall gives us guiding principles that can help us in all decisions, even those that don't seem to be specifically mentioned. Josh McDowell has written some great books to help us understand the history and the validity of the Scriptures. His book *A Ready Defense* is a great read to help one be able to answer some of the tough questions that may be asked about the overall authority of the Bible—why the Bible is true, how the Bible was composed, and many more. Helpful tools to help explain some of the more difficult to understand portions of Scripture or to help understand the context of part of Scripture can be found in commentaries, such as those online at www.biblegateway.com, www.crosswalk.com, and www.preceptaustin.org. I think we have to admit that we don't always have the answers, but it is important to explore and search with those we are investing in to help them discover that questions are part of the process. Helping one to discover how to search the Scriptures themselves goes along with the age old adage: "Give a man a fish, and he'll have food for a day. Teach a man to fish, and he'll have food for a lifetime." One of the helpful things to remember is we are all on this journey together. None of us have everything in life all figured out, and it is helpful to admit that. The younger generations desire authenticity. They already know we don't have it all figured out; they just want us to admit it.

I have found over the years, the more I have read and familiarized myself with the road atlas when I travel, the easier it is to understand it and know which direction to go. I travel a lot in my current job, and my wife and little three-year-old often travel with me. My three-year-old likes to get one of the big road atlases and look at it while she is sitting in her car seat. Now you and I both know that she really doesn't understand that map; but over time, if she keeps looking at it and getting instruction on how to read it, she will eventually be able to tell us which direction to take to get where we need to go. I remember when I was young and looked at a road atlas, it was difficult to figure it out. But now with experience and more familiarity, I am able to read most of them proficiently. Are there some maps that seem complicated to me? Absolutely, but usually with patient instruction and practice reading the map, I am able to decipher it and figure out where to go.

We can relate this concept to God's words to us in the Bible. We may not understand all of what it says to us right away, but there are some things to remember that are helpful when training in Scripture:

1. **Scripture is a guide or road map from God to help guide us in our decisions**. If a decision is not in line with God's commands or contradicts one of God's principles, then we are going a wrong direction. Just as the road atlas keeps us on the right highway, God's Word keeps us moving in the right direction. Without it we can get really far off course if we trust our feelings and our thoughts. I have more than once felt strongly while driving that I should go a certain direction, only to find out when I looked at the map I was headed in the wrong direction. The same is true of life. Feelings and instincts don't always put us on the right track, but God's word to us is always true. Helping the younger generations go to Scripture first when making decisions is a key component in spiritual formation.

2. **The Holy Spirit guides us when we read Scripture**. If training in Scripture is left out of the spiritual formation process, then it leaves out one of the main components of God's speaking to us through his Holy Spirit in Scripture. There are numerous scriptures about the role of the Holy Spirit. John 14:26 says that "the Holy Spirit…will teach you all things." John 15:26 calls the Holy Spirit " the Spirit of truth." The Holy Spirit helps guide and speak to us as we read God's words to us.

3. **The discovery of truth on one's own is much stronger than truth told by another person**. This is critical when we don't have those trusted mentor voices around us telling us which way to go and when we are in situations in which many different voices are telling us to go in different directions. If I choose something or find out something because I discovered or experienced it, it is much better and deeper than having someone tell me about it. For example, recently I went to a restaurant that had been featured on the Travel Channel's *Man v. Food*. Everyone said the

place had great food, especially a hamburger called the Big Ugly that was twenty-two ounces before cooking and one pound when it was cooked and served on a huge bun. If you eat it, you get your picture on the wall. Sure I'd heard that the food was good and the hamburger was huge, but I wasn't totally convinced. After going, seeing the Big Ugly, tasting it, and downing it (picture on the wall!), I now can tell you from experience that it is a huge burger and the place has great food. When I hear the name of that restaurant, I can speak from experience. It is different than when I had just heard about it. Now I have experienced it. The same can be said when we help younger generations experience God's Word for themselves; they experience God speaking to them through Scripture rather than being just told about Scripture.

4. **Reading Scripture is like checking in with the commander.** I have a brother-in-law who used to be in an elite branch of the secret service. Do you think that they showed up to work daily and did their thing without checking in with the commander in charge to find out the plan for that day? Or do you think those in the special forces who are extensively trained just do whatever they want? Of course not, they check in with the commander in charge to get instructions. The same can be said of our impor-tance of diving into Scripture. How do we expect to know which direction to go without first checking in to get instruction from our commander? For the majority of us, we don't hear an audible voice from God, but God has given us his words and the promise that the Holy Spirit will help guide us as we read those words.

Practically, how does this take place? How do we train in Scrip-ture those we are investing time in? Again, many things that have the biggest impact are simple steps. One way is to look at Scripture together. Encourage the person you are investing in to read a certain passage of Scripture, which you then discuss together. Some simple questions to explore are:

- ▶ What is this passage saying to you?

- ▶ How does this relate to your life?

- ▶ What are some practical things that you can do today to apply this scripture to how you live?

You could read passages or books of the Bible and then come back and talk about them. Helping those you are investing in to get familiar with and search the Scriptures for God's truth is critical in passing the baton of faith. There are numerous translations of Scripture that help put God's Word into our everyday language. Some versions I find helpful in my study are the New Living Translation, New International Version, and the New Century Version. There are numerous other versions; the most popular ones are compared in a chart at the Zondervan Bibles website[1]; this may help you figure out which one best fits you.

There's another way to help train a person in Scripture. When you are asked for advice or are exploring the future direction for the person you are investing in, simply ask, "Why don't we see what Scripture says about this?" If you don't know where to go right there at that moment, both of you could do some research in the Bible on the topic. Many Bibles have a concordance, dictionary, or index of key words in the back with scripture references. This helps the Bible become like a natural truth road map.

Other helpful ways to get scripture to become a part of everyday life is to memorize scripture. Often challenging the person you are investing in to memorize scripture that relates or helps them in certain areas of their life that may be a struggle or where they may need encouragement and direction. This helps the Bible become a natural road map that can be relied on for constant direction.

---

1. www.zondervan.com/m/bibles/translation_chart_poster.pdf

If we can get those in the younger generations to rely on Scripture for guidance in their lives, just as we rely on our GPS or road atlas, and they really become a generation who **GETS IT**, the change that would take place in our communities and around the world would be astounding. "For the word of God is living and active. Sharper than any double-edged sword, it penetrates even to dividing soul and spirit, joints and marrow; it judges the thoughts and attitudes of the heart" (Heb 4:12).

Application Questions

1. How well do you study and implement what you learn from the Bible?

2. Recall a time when God spoke to you through Scripture. How did that affect your life?

3. Dr. Stephenson says, "The discovery of truth on one's own is much stronger than truth told by another person." How have you seen this principle demonstrated?

4. Do you think it is important for you to help other believers learn to study and follow the teachings of Scripture? Why or why not?

5. What can you do to train others to rely on Scripture for guidance?

Chapter Seven

Running a Race with Focus

INTENTIONAL TIME

What if there were a type of investment guaranteed to give you unbelievable returns and incredible rewards? Most of us would want to jump on board. We often hear about financial investments that try to claim this; get-rich-quick schemes are everywhere, but in reality there are no guarantees. I was unfortunately lured into one of those claims when I was young and ended up losing $1,000. That may be pocket change to some, but to me—especially at that time in my life—$1,000 was quite a lot of money to have one day and not have the next. There may be no guarantees when it comes to financial investments, but I do believe there is a type of investment that always has a solid return. Yet many of us don't take the time to invest and reap the rewards.

Many of us live in our suburban communities, drive in and out of our garages, and pass our neighbors without even recognizing them or, if we do, we often barely know them. We unknowingly live relationally deprived lives. It is almost like people living in poverty on the wrong side of the tracks. If they have never experienced anything different, they don't know they are living in poverty. Then one day they go to a friend's house on the other side of the tracks, a friend who lives with plenty. It is only then that the one living in poverty recognizes their own situation.

Not too long ago I was living in relational poverty myself. I was successful by human standards. I interacted with hundreds of people yearly, was respected by most, had a wall full of degrees, usually talked and worked with numerous people, accomplished a lot of tasks, was disciplined, but lived relationally deprived. The saddest part was that I didn't even recognize it until I started spending time with someone who lived in relational abundance. It was like seeing the other side of the tracks .

I had a ton of acquaintances, but I always kept people at arm's length. It was the result of a combination of fear and selfishness. There was fear that if people knew the real me, they wouldn't respect me, and fear that if people really knew how messy I was inside, they wouldn't love me. These are fears that many of us share. I was selfish in that it was easier to deal with just me, because when I just have to deal with me, at least I wouldn't be disappointed or get hurt. I was selfish in that I saw investing in other people as tedious, unpredictable, and messy work. I was selfish in that with just me, I had control over what I did, or at least I thought I did. Then one day I experienced real relationship, deep relationship. The kind of relationship that caused me to ask, "What have I been missing all these years?" It was almost like discovering what a good steak tasted like after never having eaten meat.

Many of us talk a lot about relationships, but how many close friends do you have? Count them up, friends that you could call at any time, day or night. How many people can you talk to about things other than surface issues? How many individuals do you have in your life that you can go deep with and talk about the innermost part of your soul, your weaknesses, your fears, your failures? If we start to describe relationships like this, the number of friends starts to shrink, especially for men—many of us get a big fat zero.

In our current culture, relationship building isn't always seen as a positive. In the work world we are rewarded for our accomplishments and getting the job done. We aren't rewarded for building good relationships. I'm not saying we should quit working and drink coffee all day, but there is something we need to examine when we read Scripture and understand how Jesus lived.

Jesus was about thirty years old when he started his ministry. He had approximately three years to accomplish his mission, and unlike us, he knew he only had three years. Now some of us would have designed a three-year strategy to figure out a way to preach to the masses three or four times a day on a world tour. Our motto might have been, "Life is short; preach hard." Yet if you study the Gospels, what was Jesus doing most of the time? He was building relationships with the disciples. Sure he preached to the masses, but the majority of his ministry life was about building relationships.

I used to think that every minute of my day had to be scheduled to do a task; if I didn't, I would be wasting time. I used to schedule my days off with tasks. Sitting around talking would have been the ultimate waste of time. I was a student of time management, and I wanted to make sure I mastered it. I did it well and got a lot done, but what I did was live in poverty—relational poverty.

But tasting relational abundance and really getting to know people and their dreams and what was really inside their hearts gave me a taste for more. Before, in my relational poverty, I had hardly even stepped foot in a coffee house, but Starbucks is no longer a foreign land to me. I had never let people get to know the real me. Now, I let people into the messy parts of my life. And guess what, people still respect me. In fact, they say they respect me more for being real. I now understand that the true waste of time is not the investment in people; in fact, the true waste may be getting my to-do list done and being such a good time manager at the expense of good people time. God worked to help me see interruptions not as a curse but as a gift. I am actually writing this late at night at home because I went to a coffee house to write and ended up talking to a God-appointed interruption for over an hour!

We are created to be in relationship, deep relationship. Does it mean that all relationships are going to go smoothly? Of course not, some relationships are messy and some hurt deeply. Yet relationships cause us to grow, and it seems as if the messy ones often are the ones that cause us to grow the most. Without relationships we become selfish, ingrown, inward, and stunted in our growth. When people look back over their lives, the things that are usually remembered and valued aren't the tasks they checked off their list but the good times and positive relationships that they developed with people.

The past two generations understand this relationship principle well (the busters and mosaics or millennials). The majority have seen their parents work and accomplish much, but often deep relationships have been absent in their parents' lives and especially between them and their children. The youngest two generations seem to understand community and being in each other's lives much better. Why do you think coffee houses have become so popular? They want places to talk, to be real and authentic. They want people who will let them into their lives and not pretend to have it all together. They want people who will let them in on the messy parts of their lives. These generations want those who will let them wrestle with tough questions without giving canned answers.

My wife Candace is an example of this. When she was a single musician living in Nashville, she was at Starbucks almost every evening of the week, meeting new people and talking with old friends. A community developed from those who visited this particular coffee house. Some regulars even had labels. One guy who was a regular was even called the mayor of Starbucks. Now these individuals didn't keep coming to Starbucks because they wanted to pay $4 for a cup of coffee; they could have had coffee at home for much less. They came for the community and for the relational experience. Candace is incredible at getting people to open up. She could get you to talk about your deepest parts within thirty minutes—things that you may have never shared or only shared at rare times in your life. Why? Because she is so real and authentic, not afraid to talk about her own junk while always listening and remaining compassionate when you tell her yours. I think all of us yearn for that, a place where we can talk about who we really are and can just be loved.

A recent commercial tried to convince me that their mutual funds were a good choice for me to invest in for the future. We spend hours poring over information to make sure we are investing wisely in our financial future or which car to buy or which television is the best deal, but many of us spend little or no time planning how we are going to invest in the most important things in life: relationships. And to take that further, very seldom do we have *intentional* plans to invest in the younger generations around us.

In our current culture, we are pushed to accomplish. How can we accomplish more at work, more at home, more even in our leisure activities? We are rewarded for how much we can do and check off. We aren't rewarded for investing in relationships; in fact, we may even be penalized for doing so. Those who work vocationally in churches are often not exempt from this same pressure.

I was just talking to a longtime employee of a medical organization. The organization does its job well and is rated well, but it has a hard time keeping employees or getting new employees to apply. I asked, "Do you think the supervisors value or care about the personal life of the people that work for them?" His answer told me what I had suspected. The answer was, "No, they don't care if you come back or not; they just want the job done." Unfortunately, this isn't an extreme case; it happens often in the business world and even in some of our ministry organizations.

Relational time often isn't seen as being productive. The gadgets that were created to make our lives easier have made our lives busier. In less developed countries, as well as decades ago in the United States, it could be argued that talking around the fire or on the front porch was a way of life, far more than a once-in-a-blue-moon occurrence. I am not saying we should go back to outdoor plumbing, but I am saying we need to examine our strategies for investing time.

Many of us invest in many things. Some of us are wise financially and invest in IRAs, pensions, college funds, and savings. Some of us invest in our careers by spending significant time and energy trying to move to the next level. Some of us invest in watching television; some homes have them on almost every hour that someone is at home. (I challenge you to keep a log of how many hours your television is on for one week, I think you will be surprised.) Some of us invest in our hobbies, spending incredible amounts of time and money on these pursuits. The list goes on and on. In Matthew 6:21, Jesus says, "For where your treasure is, there your heart will be also."

It is often amazing how often we are surprised that the things we didn't invest in don't turn out the way we wanted. For example, parents who convinced themselves that working extra was for their children's good so they could give them more material possessions are astonished when their teenage son or daughter rebels. Or parents who allow the television to be the teacher of their children wonder why their children don't hold godly views of life. It is interesting how we hold principles in some areas but not others. For example, those with financial wisdom know that if you save just a little bit every month for years in a compound-interest-bearing account, that money will grow to a great sum. Or again, many of us know that if we invest extra time at the office every day for months or years, it often is the next step to promotion. Yet we often fail to apply this principle to people. If we invest just a little time in others, it can be life changing for them and for us, especially when that investment is in the younger generations.

I am a firm believer that what you do consistently—little by little—will make a big difference. For example, if you are twenty-five years old and you gain just two pounds a year, about a half an ounce a week (yes, you read that right, a half an ounce), by the time you are fifty, you will be fifty pounds heavier than you are now. You may be saying, "You don't have to tell me; I am living proof!" The same can be said when it comes to investments of time.

Remember our earlier spiritual formation process:

GETS IT = Spiritual Formation

As we talked about in the previous chapters, a key component of passing the baton is living a life that asks key questions: How close can I get to Jesus and what is he saying to me? How can I help others discover God's roadmap for themselves? The other component is how we invest our time. What we do little by little makes a big difference in relationships and is a key factor in how we pass the baton to the next generations. Investing intentional time and saying encouraging words to those around us, especially the younger generations, matter. Words are powerful.

We often remember positive and negative things that are said to us. For example, when I was about eleven years old, I was playing baseball. I was about to step into the batter's box against a pitcher who was one of the best in the league. He was a man playing with boys. This kid was developed, muscular, and here I was: this scrawny eleven year old nervous to even step to the plate. My dad was at the game, and as I was on deck about to face Goliath, Dad came over to the fence and told me that I could get a hit on him, that I could even hit a home run off of him. To be honest, I was just hoping not to be taken to the hospital by being hit by one of his pitches. But something happened when my dad believed in me. I somehow got the bat on the ball and hit it over the fence. That is a great memory of someone believing in me. I also remember another time where I received a negative image of myself, a very simple offhanded remark at age twelve or thirteen from one of my older relatives saying that I was going to have to watch it or I would get fat. From that day on I promised myself that would never happen. All of us can bring up words or things that were said to us that have shaped us positively or negatively. I know that having someone older say just a word of encouragement or invest a little time in me has made a huge impact in my life.

What would happen if every person who has a relationship with Jesus Christ invested just a little time in a person who is younger than they are? How many successful baton passes would we have? What would happen if just one hour were invested in that person each week? Over a year, that would be 52 hours; over two years, 104 hours; and over four years, over 208 hours. I used to teach as an adjunct professor in a university setting. Over the course of about fourteen weeks, we would spend about thirty-six hours in class for a three-hour credit. So over two years, investing in someone just one hour a week would be like taking almost three college courses.

You may be thinking, "Where am I going to find an extra hour a week? I am already so busy I can barely keep up!" We may be busy, but busy doesn't always mean we are making a difference, and usually it doesn't mean we don't have any room in our schedule. If I may be so bold, it is probably because we haven't examined our priorities. If we really want our life to count, and I am assuming this is true or you wouldn't be reading this book, we have to step back and examine our priorities.

I am amazed at how many people who have spent all the money they made, without a strong savings plan, are surprised when they reach fifty or sixty years of age to find that they don't have enough money saved up for retirement. Or the person who doesn't exercise and eats unhealthy foods for decades is surprised they have a heart attack at age fifty. Or the dad who works late every night is surprised when his kids are eighteen and don't have a close relationship with him. Making your life count doesn't happen in a day or all at once. It is an incremental process that happens over a lifetime. Thinking you can wait until you get to a certain age and then you will make a difference is almost as crazy as saying I will wait and start saving for retirement when I retire. Start now and remember this principle: a little bit goes a long way.

What I have found is that we spend our time on what we value most. Most of us work at a paying job because we value having money to live. Some of us work certain jobs or hours because we want a certain lifestyle. Most of us do things in our schedule because we value that activity. Sure, there are times we may not be able to do the things we love, but if we really value something, sooner or later we will work it into our schedule. Television, fantasy sports leagues, golf, shopping, movies, sports, hunting, fishing and the list goes on—if it is a priority, we will find the time for it.

Think about this: If you watch television just three hours a day, which is lower than the national average for the typical household in the United States, in one year you will have invested more than 1,095 hours watching television. In five years you would have invested 5,475 hours, and in ten years, 10,950 hours. Let's break that down. In ten years, if you watched television just three hours a day, you would have spent a total of 456 full twenty-four-hour days (that is a full year plus ninety-one days watching television day and night). That also equates to 1,368 eight-hour days (3.75 years of eight-hour days)! The typical full-time job, working five days a week and taking off for vacation and holidays has us working eight hours a day for 250 days a year. So if you watch television for just three hours a day over a ten-year period, it would be the equivalent of working a full-time job for almost five and a half years! Too bad television doesn't pay us for watching. To put it differently, you would have spent the amount of time you would have to spend in class for a four-year college degree in watching television after just a couple of years if you watched just three hours a day. You may be thinking, "I wish I had known that, it would have saved me a fortune in school loans!"

If you only watch 1.5 hours a day, much less than the typical person, you will have invested over 547 hours in a year, 2,737 hours in five years, and 5,475 hours in ten years. In ten years, that's a total of 228 full twenty-four-hour days or 684 eight-hour days (almost two full years of eight hour days) at just 1.5 hours a day. It is pretty staggering when you think about it.

Hear me, I am not saying watching television is wrong. What I am saying is that we might need to take a closer look at our priorities. Some may be saying, "I don't watch that much television." Great, but it may be something else, such as shopping, fantasy leagues, time on the computer, or time on Facebook. I have to be careful; I love sports and the outdoors. I need to make sure that I don't value those more than investing in others. However we spend our time, we need to examine our lives and our priorities. What can I do that will make a difference? If we don't have an hour a week to give to invest in someone younger than we are to make a difference, we probably need to reexamine our values and our priorities.

It doesn't take much. A little time here and a little there goes a long way. Don't wait until you can carve out a large block of time, because for 95% of us, that block of time will never happen. Spontaneity is great, but for most, a dream does not come true without

planning. We often overestimate what we can do in a short time period and underestimate what we can do over longer periods. Where
it happens is a little here and a little there, and before we know it,
our time investment has grown more than we ever imagined. Even
if we invested just thirty minutes a week, over a year that is twenty-
six hours, more than half of a work week! In ten years it would add
up to thirty-two eight-hour days. Think of this, just fifteen minutes
a day adds up to ninety-one hours a year (almost four full days and
nights!). A little goes a long way.

The real question for most reading this book is what do we want
to invest in that will make a difference? How can I make my life
count? What are we going to do that will last?

If we are going to pass the baton well, we have to be intentional
in planning how we are going to spend our time in order to make
that happen. Just hoping it happens won't make it happen. What
do we need to do to shift some things in our lives to make sure we
have what is most important first? What is something you can do
that would help in passing the baton off well to the next generation,
even if it is just five minutes a day (that would add up to thirty-five
minutes a week)?

What will they say about us, that we spent intentional time on the
track running and passing the baton well or that we were too busy
and consumed with other things that we never even thought about
it? Just remember, a little amount of time makes a big difference and
one word of encouragement can help change a destiny.

Application Questions

1. Name someone who has invested time in your spiritual growth. In what specific ways did that person make a difference to you?

2. Dr. Stephenson notes that our Western culture is task driven versus relationship driven. How does this affect our approach to Christian discipleship?

3. Which has brought more joy to your life—possessions or relationships? Explain.

4. When you considered the ways you spend your time, how did it make you feel? Are there some areas you need to adjust your investment of time?

5. What positive words has someone spoken to you that really made a difference in your life?

Chapter Eight

Making Smooth Hand Offs

PASSING THE BATON TO THE YOUNGER GENERATIONS
So how do we make our lives count? Do we measure our life by how many titles or degrees we have? Or by how much money we make? Sure, titles, degrees, and even money can be a venue for us to make a difference, but these things we had are soon forgotten. Just try to remember who won the World Series four years ago or who played in the Super Bowl ten years ago. Can you? Who won the gold medal in the 100-meter event two Olympics ago or who won the Academy Award for best actor eight years ago? Can you name the best picture four years ago or name five of the top one hundred richest people ten years ago? Without doing some research, many of us have trouble naming even one or two.

Living a life that makes a difference isn't about awards or fame or how much money you have when you die. Fame fades; money fades; awards rust. First Corinthians 13:8 talks about what will last: "Love never fails. But where there are prophecies, they will cease; where there are tongues, they will be stilled; where there is knowledge, it will pass away." Most of us will leave a lot of stuff behind when we die. Some of us will leave a lot of money, and others a lot of items accumulated. Just recently I was sorting numerous books and other items left in the basement by my wife's grandfather, who passed away quite a few years ago. In reality, most of those books were out of date and weren't useful today. But what is powerful wasn't the stuff that was left (most of it was given or thrown away); it is the legacy of faith that my wife's grandfather passed to his children, his grandchildren, and now—even though he isn't around—to his great-grandchildren.

You wouldn't be reading this book if you didn't want to make a difference. You wouldn't have gotten this far if you didn't want to pass the baton of faith smoothly. So how does one pass the baton of faith? How does one leave a lasting legacy?

GETS IT = Spiritual Formation

In the examples of Jesus and the disciples, Moses and Joshua, Naomi and Ruth, Paul and Timothy, Elijah and Elisha, you can see this biblical process of spiritual formation being lived out. If you take a closer look at these relationships, they are investing in those who are younger than they are. If Jesus and the others listed above left lasting legacies by investing in those who were younger than they were, shouldn't we follow suit? If that was the Son's plan for his limited time here on earth, wouldn't it make sense that it should be our plan if we really want to live a life that makes a difference and sets up a smooth hand off?

What are some practical steps we can take if we really want to make a difference with our life? This chapter will give practical suggestions and help to get your creative juices flowing so that you can develop your own plan to make a difference and pass the baton well.

For those of us who are parents and grandparents, our first responsibility of spiritual formation is to our own children and grandchildren. We can't be like an Eli (1 Sam 2), who was so focused on ministry that he lost his children in the process. What can we do to make sure we pass the baton of faith well? How do we start? Often when we think about things like this, we get overwhelmed and think we need numerous hours and a sophisticated system. Yet typically the most powerful spiritual formation comes in simple day-to-day living. One way to pass the baton well is as simple as modeling it by your example of making God the priority in your life and home. Many Christians feel that bringing God or spiritual things into a regular conversation seems contrived or forced, largely because many Christians reserve discussion of spiritual things for Sunday mornings. Why? Why can we talk to our children about school, sports, the weather, or what is on the menu for dinner with an ease and naturalness, while discussing spiritual things seems awkward, boring, and forced? Part of the process of spiritual formation is making God and spiritual things a natural part of conversation. Here are some ideas to help you:

► Pray with your children, not just at meals but every morning or every night. Pray during the day. Stop and pray and thank God for everyday things. Ask him for direction when you have to make a decision. When your kids are sick or have big decisions, stop and pray. Make prayer a regular conversation like you would have with another family member. For example, recently my three-year-old and I were taking my wife to the airport very early in the morning. On the way home she saw a school bus and commented on it. It was the first day of school for many in our area, so I said let's pray for those students going to school, and while we were driving, I prayed for students and for their year. Simple, yes, but I want her to know that prayer is a natural part of life.

► Make spiritual conversation a normal part of discussion. For example, after a message at a worship service, ask your children what they heard God saying to them. If they are younger, ask what they learned about God today and what they heard him saying during class time.

► Pray with them before they go to school. Here is one idea I heard recently when talking to a friend. Before school each morning, they pray as a family, with each person taking a section and praying on the armor of God found in Ephesians 6:10–17.

► Make Scripture a natural part of life. Memorize scripture together. Have it featured on your refrigerator. Have a theme scripture in large letters you read before you leave the house. One of my friends designed scripture cards on a ring binder that flip so that his kids could read them as they brush their teeth. Make Scripture a regular part of the family.

▶ Make turning to God a natural part of decision making. Ask questions like, What do you think God would want you (us) to do? What do you think Jesus would do? If the children are a little older, look at scriptures that might apply to the situation. For example, there are many stories about standing up courageously for one's belief (e.g., Daniel, Noah, Esther); there are many sayings of Jesus about how to treat others and deal with relationships. If we can help Scripture become a part of the decision-making process while kids are young, it will help them rely on it to make wise decisions as they get older.

▶ Read Scripture or Bible story books with your children. Ask about the main principle or main message of the story. If you have younger children, make this a fun time, perhaps by letting them act some of the story out. There are numerous Bible story books available in your local bookstore. (*Egermeier's Bible Story Book* is a great one. See the appendix.) Some families do this nightly, others weekly. If you are thinking about implementing this with your children, note that it may be easier to start slowly once or twice a week and increase the frequency over time.

▶ Tell stories to younger children that revolve around a godly principle. For example, Galatians 5:22–23 talks about the fruit of the Spirit: "But the fruit of the Spirit is love, joy, peace, patience, kindness, goodness, faithfulness, gentleness and self-control. Against such things there is no law." You could tell stories you make up about a particular fruit of the Spirit each week. For example, I tell my three-year-old stories about kindness and treating all people kindly no matter what they look like. I want her to understand how God wants us to live. With older kids, you might just ask them if they have lived out a fruit of the Spirit today and talk about it at the dinner table. Of course, you should be the one who starts the conversation and models how you have lived or have not lived out a fruit of the Spirit that day in order to spur the discussion as a family.

▶ Let them see you model consistent time in prayer and reading Scripture alone with God. Growing up, there were few mornings when I didn't see my mom on the couch having her time with Jesus. Her consistent example was powerful. Like it or not, most of our children will pick up and model much of what we do or don't do. Our abundance of time with the Father, or lack thereof, will often be duplicated.

▶ Make prayer and thankfulness a natural part of your life, not some formal thing. If something is going well, say out loud, "God thank you for…." Or if there is a situation, stop and pray right then. You can pray while you are in the car; God doesn't care if our eyes are open or closed. As children get older, don't be afraid to talk about the hard questions of faith. Don't act surprised if they seem to be going a different direction; help them own their faith by helping them work it through. Don't say, "I can't believe you are saying or thinking that!" Sometimes kids will say things to see how we are going to react; deep down they want to see if we will still love them no matter what. Our spiritual life is often messy. I would rather be there to go through the messy times with my kids than have some stranger helping them process life decisions while they are away at college. The spiritual journey is a process, and there are often detours along the way. In these times, kids need us to help them process.

If the church is living as the community God designed it to be, parents who are godly ought to be able to count on the church to help them disciple their children. They ought to be able to count on others to come alongside them by intentionally spending time, living as Godly examples, and training them in Scripture—being a major part of the **GETS IT** process. For those in our churches who don't have godly parents, we are their only hope.

Whether you have children or not, we should all be investing in someone younger than we are. Our children and grandchildren should be our first priority if we have them, but we should also have someone other than our children and grandchildren in whom we are investing. Whatever age you are, whether you are fourteen or ninety, God has called you to invest in someone who is younger than you are. It could be someone who is fifty if you are sixty, or someone who is twelve if you are sixteen. If you are in junior high, it could be an elementary-age student. God has designed us to pass the baton. Just as in Matthew 25:14–28 when the master gave one servant five talents, another two, and another one, God has called us to invest in someone else with whatever he has given us, to live out God's purpose for us.

In theory all of this sounds great. In practicality, let's face it, it is a little scary for some of us, and to be honest it can be messy and it takes time. If it were an easy task, we wouldn't face the leadership vacuum we are facing today in our churches. Investing in others truly only happens with intentionality. Before we talk about things we can do, let's look at some of the obstacles that hold us back. Identifying obstacles and how we can overcome them can be freeing.

One of the greatest obstacles we face is fear. The enemy does such a great job of using fear to paralyze us. One fear is that we don't have anything to offer. Maybe you feel you aren't really a leader. Or maybe you are thinking, "I don't have this God thing figured out myself, so how can I pour into someone else?" You have doubts in your own life, so you wonder how can you help someone else. The enemy is so good at causing us to look at what we can't do to keep us from doing what we can do. The issue shouldn't be about us and what we can and can't do but about how God wants to use us.

David Ring is a great example of this. David is a nationally known Christian speaker who has cerebral palsy. When you listen to him, you have to listen closely and intently to understand what he is saying through his garbled words. If he came to your church, you might wonder what you'd got yourself into when he started to speak, because he is so hard to understand. But David is one who allows God to use him with what God gave him. Instead of dwelling on what he can't do, he instead lets God use him to make a difference. He speaks to more than one hundred thousand people annually in churches, schools, conventions, and corporate events, and God uses him to make a difference in many lives. God can use us with whatever he has given us.

Another fear leaders sometimes have is the fear of giving up their position or title. I was with some leaders on another continent and we challenged them to invest in others. In a show of absolute honesty, they verbalized that they feared losing their positions if they poured themselves into younger leaders. Westerners aren't much different; we worry about that same issue, but typically we aren't honest enough to say it; we just live it out by doing everything ourselves and holding onto power. Some time back, I heard about a senior pastor of a fairly large church who was so involved in micromanaging and holding onto power that he was even involved in the details of which pens were bought and how far the tables should be spaced apart for set up (he actually measured them). I am sure he could have found qualified people to take care of those details and helped them to use their talents and gifts. When we give people power to lead and use their gifts, often the opposite of what we fear happens: people are more loyal and more appreciative of our leadership than ever. We also live out God's purpose of helping people be who and what God has called them to be when we give them the freedom and opportunities to do so.

Fear can also cause us to hold back from starting things, keeping us from experiencing all that God has for us. Often when we push through our fears, we get to experience incredible moments. A few years ago, my wife and I snorkeled in the Bahamas. We came to a place where our guides said there were many sharks below us, and if we wanted, we could get in the water by holding onto a rope attached to the boat that went about fifty feet out from the back. They instructed us not to release any bodily fluids and to move as little as possible, merely holding on to the rope and looking below. Swim with sharks under you and don't pee in your pants, try that! I was nervous; I was in open water with sharks. If you have seen the classic movie *Jaws* or the Discovery Channel's *Shark Week*, you can relate. I jumped into the water as lightly as a two-hundred-pound-plus person can jump and held onto the rope. Sure enough, there were numerous sharks just below us. It was incredible watching them. One shark came a little too close for comfort toward me, yet we made it back into the boat with all our body parts intact! After everyone was back in the boat, the guides started throwing some fish scraps they had brought off the back of the boat. The shark feeding frenzy was incredible. Did I experience some fear before I got in the water? Sure! But overcoming it allowed me to experience one of the coolest things I have ever done. The same is true of pushing through some of our fears of investing in people. Sure it can be scary and we rarely know how it is going to end, but the rewards of experiencing God's great purpose far outweigh the costs.

Fear isn't the only hindrance when it comes to investing in others. We are often hindered by the lack of time in our schedules. You may be thinking, "I don't have any room in my schedule to invest in someone! I am maxed out!" I am sometimes relieved when I travel to developing countries and see how laid back they are with their time. They may have something on those of us living in North America because there people don't get stressed out if someone shows up a little off schedule. Over the years I have noticed something in my own life and when working with others: we spend time doing what is important to us. Sure there are times when we may not get to do what is important to us for a season, but if it is truly important, we will find time. Our schedules reflect what is important to us. So maybe we shouldn't say, "I don't have time," maybe we should say, "That isn't important to me," "I didn't make that a priority," or "I didn't make time for that." When we really believe in something, we adjust our schedules in almost all cases.

If you were driving down the highway and there were obstacles in the road, you would have to detour to get to where you needed to go. You would reroute your vehicle and find another way to get to your destination. In the same way, we need to recognize that there will be obstacles as we try to pass the baton in various seasons of life, things that make intentionally investing time in passing the baton harder. Yet the important thing is making sure that even with the detours of life, we stay on the course and keep running the race.

You may be thinking, "I want to invest in someone younger, life on life. I am willing to risk and break through the hindrances. I want to be one who helps to be a part of passing the baton to a generation that **GETS IT**. I want to live out the process (**Godly Example + Training in Scripture + Intentional Time = Spiritual Formation**), but how do I start?" The pleasant surprise is that often you don't have to alter your current schedule much. Often the best spiritual formation is done life on life; we sometimes think it has to be this formalized teaching, which is important, but often the most meaningful spiritual formation comes in informal settings.

GETS IT = Spiritual Formation

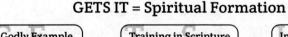

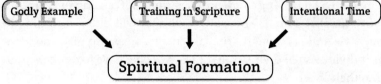

Let's do an experiment. Think for a moment. If you regularly attend a local church, you typically hear a message every Sunday. That message usually has a title and some main points associated with it. Can you name ten message titles and at least one point from each of those messages in the last year? Okay, let's expand it, can you name ten message titles and main points in the last five years? If you are having a hard time with coming up with ten, just name five of them. If you attended a small group or a Sunday school, can you remember any lesson titles in the last year? What about your lifetime? For some of us we can't even name what was taught last week! And for some of us, as teachers we may not be able to remember what we taught last month or even last week. How many points from a conference you recently attended can you recite? For the majority of us, trying to remember any of these things is difficult. On the other hand, can you name five people who have had an influence in your life? List one thing each of them did that made a difference in your life? My guess is you had to struggle to name the sermons and points, even your own, if you're a pastor or Sunday school teacher. But I would bet you came up with the people who made a difference in your life pretty fast. My guess is also that you probably didn't list a formal training setting in how they affected your life.

Below are just a few examples of how you could pour into others; these are just suggestions, not an exhaustive list. Each of us has our own personality and style, so it is better for us to take some ideas and create what works best for us and our personality rather than to try to force things that don't fit us. For example, taking someone to a sporting event when we hate sports would be a misfit, but if we loved music and took them to a concert, that would be a fit. The important thing is to help those we are investing in to be someone who **GETS IT (Living as a Godly Example + Training in Scripture + Intentional Time)**. The way we do that will differ according to our style and personality. The last chapter may also give you ideas as individuals tell their stories of ways people have had others pour into their lives.

One of the easiest ways to pour into another is to ask someone to accompany you somewhere, whether it is to the store, a hospital visit, going to coffee, your kid's ballgame, a sports event, graduation, you name it. Incorporating someone into what you are already doing is a great way to intentionally spend time. This gives them a chance to see you in real life and how you relate to your family and others as well as fitting someone else into your regular rhythm of life.

Inviting someone to help you with a project is another great way to invest. Often the best coaching comes by just being with others. I remember having one of my students come help me with some landscaping projects and having some good conversations as we worked. It can also help build some skills they wouldn't ever learn unless someone showed them. I personally have learned some skills in this setting with others a little younger than me, as well as having some good bonding time.

Another great way to intentionally invest is to invite someone over to have a meal with you and your family. This is often a very powerful time, especially for the younger generation who often hasn't seen family modeled well. The impact that this can have on a younger person is tremendous—just exposing them to a functional, loving family opens their eyes to the way God intends us to live. When all they've seen are unhealthy interactions, it is a big deal for them to see that there is hope for their future to be different from the way they were raised.

Another way to invest is to have a regular or weekly meeting time with them. What these times entail varies. For some it involves meeting once a week, for others once a month, for others once every two months. You have to find what works for you. You could spend this time talking about life, studying what the Bible says about life topics, or studying portions of Scripture. You could study an inspiring book together, or a combination of all of these. The important thing is the intentional time. You will find some suggestions for Bible study and book studies in the appendix.

Another way to intentionally invest time is by sending a text, a Facebook message, a letter, or by giving them a phone call. Checking in to see how they are doing, letting them know you are praying for them and that you care for them can be very powerful. The people who have invested in me have sent such messages, and they have been fuel for my soul and seem to come at just the right time. They typically don't take a lot of time, but they can make an incredible impact in a person's life. One thing I have found is they usually only happen if they are intentionally scheduled on my calendar.

Here is a short recap:

- ▶ Take someone with you—the store, a hospital visit, ballgame, wherever.

- ▶ Incorporate someone into a project you are doing.

- ▶ Have someone over for a meal.

- ▶ Take someone out for coffee.

- ▶ Meet with someone regularly—every week, every other week, once a month.

- ▶ Text, message, write, or call someone to encourage them.

To really influence and make a difference, those we invest in must know that we really know and care for them. People want to be known. This usually doesn't come through some formal process, but just by getting to know a person—knowing about their family, their special days (birthdays, anniversaries, etc.), what they enjoy doing, their favorite food, their favorite junk food, their favorite teams, favorite movies or television shows, where they would go if they could travel anywhere, what their dreams for the future are. Knowing and caring for them is about knowing their story, how they came to know Christ, where they grew up, about their family. Often you can find out a lot about someone by just asking them to share their story.

Here are a few questions that may help you get to really know and care for a person:

- ▶ Would you tell me your story of how you came to know Christ?

- ▶ Would you tell me about your family? If it applies, you could ask how long they have been married, when they got married, and how they met their spouse. If they have children, find out the ages of their children and ask them to talk about their children (almost everyone loves to talk about their children). If a person is not married, ask them about the family they grew up in.

▶ When is your birthday? If you want, you can find out other important dates of the family, e.g., spouse's birthday, anniversary, kids' birthdays. A text, e-mail, or call is always appreciated on a special day and shows you really care and know them. A gift certificate to a favorite store or their favorite restaurant may help to show them you know them individually.

▶ What is your favorite food and restaurant?

▶ If you could meet anyone, dead or alive, who would you want to meet?

▶ What are your hobbies or some things you like to do?

▶ What are your favorite sports teams, favorite music artists, favorite television show or movie?

▶ If you could go anywhere in the world, where would you travel?

The bottom line is that God has given all of us a baton to pass to those running behind us. Whatever way we choose to do it and whatever creative ways God gives us, we have a responsibility to make a smooth hand off.

As was noted in chapter five, living our life as a godly example is a key part of passing the baton. Just recently I was talking to someone about a high profile leader who failed in this area and the extensive damage caused to others by his behavior. Remember, those you are investing in will be watching how you live. All of the three elements are critical in the spiritual formation process: living as a Godly Example, Training in Scripture, and investing Intentional Time. Leaving out one of these is like leaving out a main ingredient in a recipe or a key piece of the puzzle. We need all three. Keep running, stay on course, and pass the baton well. The next generations are counting on you.

Application Questions

1. What type of legacy do you want to leave to the generations that follow you?

2. If you are a parent or grandparent, which of Dr. Stephenson's recommendations would you like to implement to pass the baton to your children or grandchildren? What other ideas come to mind?

3. Which obstacle more often prevents you from sharing your faith with someone else: fear or lack of time? How might you overcome that?

4. Are you investing your time and attention in discipling someone who is younger than you? If you can't identify a specific person, write down the names of one or two persons that you could disciple and begin praying about how you will pass the baton of faith on to them.

5. Review the practical suggestions of how you could make a smooth hand off of your faith. What suggestion stood out to you? What can you do to implement that suggestion in the next two weeks?

Chapter Nine

A Call to Church Leaders

PASSING THE BATON TO THE YOUNGER GENERATIONS
The last chapter was directed to anyone who has a relationship with Jesus Christ, no matter what their age. The mission: pass the baton well. This chapter is designed specifically for those who consider themselves leaders in the church. This section addresses how to pass the baton as a church leader and how to help create a culture of passing the baton in your congregation. Passionate spiritual leadership is often related to intentional discipleship. Even if you are not currently in a leadership role in your congregation, you may gain something from this chapter, but since your eighth grade English teacher is no longer breathing down your neck, don't hesitate to skip it!

Now, if you are like most church leaders, you often have numerous individuals that you manage and interact with in your daily life. You probably find yourself short on time and stretched too thin in your emotional bandwidth. I understand the pressure, having been in full-time vocational ministry for over two decades and also having grown up in a pastor's home. I have experienced the demands of being a leader and the child of a leader in the church. There are a lot of demands and expectations put on most church leaders, often keeping us involved in damage control rather than making a difference. For church leaders, handing off the baton is imperative. When a leader steps down or moves on, it is far too common for the ministry they were overseeing to decline or be eliminated. In most cases, there wasn't a smooth hand off of the baton. We have to start thinking about setting up the next generation to lead well. It has to be in the forefront of our mind, not just when we know we are about to leave but as a part of our leadership culture. We always have to be thinking about setting up the hand off and pushing those after us to the next level.

As we all know, this doesn't happen without an investment in people. Yet how do we really invest and get to know and care for people if we have dozens, hundreds, or even thousands of people in our ministry? I wonder if Jesus felt that way; he had thousands clamoring to be near him, to touch him, to be healed by him, to talk to him. But where do we see Jesus spending the majority of his time? With his twelve disciples, and even more with the three in his inner circle. He knew all about them—their dreams, their hopes, their fears, their strengths and weaknesses. Now if God himself chose to fully invest in a smaller number rather than a multitude of people, what does that mean for us?

Passing the baton smoothly involves giving away some of our leadership and even some of the things that we may enjoy doing but that we don't necessarily need to do. In order to pass the baton well, we have to look deep into our hearts and make some wise leadership decisions. We have to be willing to not be a part of everything that goes on. We don't have to be involved in every decision, even major ones. Our role is to empower others to do ministry. A leader who is intentional about passing the baton is also intentional about helping others find God's purpose for their own lives and seeks to help them live that out. Sure, if we hand off things to others it may get done a little differently than if we did it ourselves. But a strong leader is thinking about setting up the future. If someone else we have been investing in does something and they do a better job than we do, we should celebrate. Unfortunately, this doesn't always happen; jealously often creeps in. When a younger leader gives a great message and everyone is saying how incredible it was, celebrate. When someone leads a training session and everyone is amazed at how great it was, celebrate. Let's face it, as leaders we will not be the best at everything; no human can be. Great leaders help others be all that God has designed them to be by lifting them higher and higher.

We have to be open to giving up ownership, especially to the younger generations who desire to be a part of something that makes a difference. Yet as leaders we can be too insecure to give up owner-ship. We sometimes feel that if we give ministry and responsibilities to others, it threatens our power and position. We would probably never verbalize that, but our egos often keep us from delegating responsibilities. Early in my ministry, in my immaturity, I would compete (not outwardly but inwardly) with a particular youth leader to be liked the most by the students. My insecurity hindered the ministry until God shook me and helped me realize that I should rejoice when students connected better with other leaders. Many of the students had personalities that were different from mine, and my job was to enable others to do ministry, not for me to be in the limelight. As leaders, holding onto our role or position can get in the way of what God wants to do through younger leaders.

As leaders in the church how do we help create a church culture that really **GETS IT**? How do we become a church with a culture of passing the baton well? How do we help develop passionate spiritual leaders? Deep down we all want to develop passionate spiritual leaders and hand off the baton well, but it doesn't happen without intentionality.

So where do we start? One of the first steps is to have an expecta-tion that paid and volunteer leaders are always thinking about the future. The question should constantly be asked by all leaders: How will I set up the next leader after me? We have to make sure that we are building a foundation for the next generation of leaders to move to the next level after we leave. One of the things I am always trying to emphasize to my team is for us to help set up the next generation of leaders who follow us to take the ministry to the next level. We want to pave the way for them and for the future ministry and lift them on our shoulders to reach higher than we could ever dream. I know I have done my job as a leader if after I leave, the ministry grows and moves to new heights.

How do we help the ministry move to the next level? Following the model of Jesus, we have to find and invest our lives in a few key leaders. For senior pastors, it may be your board of elders and your staff; for associates, it may be your key staff; for youth pastors, it may be your student leaders and youth leaders; and for volunteer leaders, it would be those who you oversee. It involves really getting to know them, doing life with them, letting them know you really care about them, investing in them, training and empowering them, and helping them be all God wants them to be. That means spending time with them personally, as well as encouraging them professionally. It starts by knowing their story, knowing and investing in their family, knowing their dreams, their fears, and their passions. This also means recognizing certain gifts. For example, my former boss recognized that some on the team were more gifted in certain areas than she was, so she often let different members of the team lead in their giftedness, even to the point of letting some of her staff lead the overall team meetings. By the way, she is very talented, respected by thousands, and has a knack for helping people become better.

You may be reading this and feel overwhelmed by the sheer number of people that come to mind that you oversee. How can you really get to know them at this level? The reality is you will have to make some intentional choices of how many you can truly invest in on this one-on-one level. A good rule of thumb would be to follow Jesus' example; he invested himself in twelve people, and he even narrowed that group down to his inner circle of three. So how does one do this with a large staff or a multitude of ministry leaders? This is where intentionality and the multiplication principle become essential. For example, if you have twenty persons you oversee, choose four or five of that group that you designate as team leaders. These would be the ones that you really invest in and shepherd. Set it up where they invest in and shepherd four or five members of the team of twenty. This enables you to really get to know and invest in a few and also sets up the future. If you ensure the twenty are invested in but it isn't your responsibility to personally invest in every single one, you have already set the situation up for investment to occur. Now God will be able to use others without the ministry being completely dependent on you. In doing this, you are creating an investment culture rather than a culture of dependency on personality. Ministries based on personalities usually fail or decline when the leader leaves. Great leaders set others up for the future. If we look at Jesus' ministry, we see that he set his disciples up for success when he left. He knew them, cared for them, invested in them, trained them, and empowered them by sending them out on short experiential missions before he handed them the ministry. As church leaders, we should have the same goal. We should be setting up future leaders for success. How do we do this? By knowing our leaders, caring for them, investing in them, training them and sending or releasing them to lead.

One of my responsibilities has been to direct a convention with an attendance of five thousand to seven thousand people. A couple of years ago, my boss and I realized that if we were going to set up for the future, we needed each major leader to have a person they were investing in to be able to do their job. All of the leaders over major areas were required to have an apprentice to work alongside them. Now we have it set up so that there is more than one person leading most of our main areas of ministry. As a result, if a major leader isn't able to participate any more, the ministry doesn't suffer. What if all the major ministries of our churches required someone to come alongside the current ministry director to be trained to carry the ministry on to the next level. Every ministry area from the nursery to the older adults would always have a leader investing in another leader, thinking about setting up the future. I challenge you as church leaders to build this into the culture, where it is an expectation rather than a rarity. I know that many of our churches are excited just to have someone fill a role and have a body in place to oversee an area. Churches often bemoan the fact that they are short on volunteers. I believe that if a culture of knowing and caring for others individually by doing life together, providing quality training, having high expectations and empowering others to lead in their passion and gift areas were present, it would create a different atmosphere than is found in most of our churches and volunteers may not be as hard to find. If setting up the next generation of leaders was an expectation rather than a hope, it would help sustain our ministries and help our ministry leaders not burn out.

In reality, this passing of the baton principle starts with us. A good principle to try to practice as a leader is, if possible, to take someone with you. If you are going to make a hospital visit or going somewhere to speak, take someone with you. For example, if you know there is a young person who is interested in church leadership, structure some of your visits in the afternoon or evening so that they can go along with you. One caveat, though: never take the opposite gender alone. Many church leaders violate this important principle and get into trouble. Even if it seems harmless, the enemy loves to get gossip going around that detracts from ministry. If you live by a standard that states you don't ride or spend time alone with the opposite gender who isn't your spouse or family, then you don't have to waste time dealing with accusations.

All of us would love to see all believers in our local congregations practicing spiritual formation. How do you build a culture of spiritual formation into your local church life? There are many programs and curricula about spiritual formation available to churches. I believe curriculum is important, and, as mentioned earlier, I even helped write a four-level spiritual formation series for students.[1] But if we are honest, most of our churches aren't doing a great job at producing disciples. Could it be we have been so focused on a classroom model that we have missed the life-on-life model? What if every believer in our church would see it as their calling to be a godly example, help train others in Scripture, and intentionally invest time in others? Would the number of those leaving the church, and often times turning away from God, decrease?

Investing in others would be a cultural shift in many of our churches. Often our churches are full of individuals who are more concerned about what the church can do for them than what they can do for God. Far too frequently, the current church culture in North America isn't a **GETS IT** model when it comes to spiritual formation. Spiritual formation in the form of **Godly Example + Training in Scripture + Intentional Time** represents a cultural shift for most congregations. When you study history, you realize cultural shifts don't happen overnight. They occur over time. The same is

---

1. The Ultimate Adventure series. See the appendix for further information.

true for our churches. Creating a culture of spiritual formation is going to be a process, not a quick one-time sermon series. The early church started as a discipleship church, so the cultural shift away didn't happen overnight and neither will the shift back. Paradigm and cultural shifts happen little by little. When you drive a car with a manual transmission, you don't typically shift from neutral to fifth gear. You go to first, then to second, and so on. So in our churches, it starts with faithful leaders starting to shift the momentum toward an influencing culture. It is said that a train stopped on a track can be held in place by a block of wood, but a train traveling at fifty miles an hour can run through a concrete wall. In the same way, it can be tough to get things going, but once the culture starts to shift, the change starts to gain momentum and is hard to stop.

As a church leader, there are steps you can take to begin the shift. First, you have to be fully investing in a few people yourself. You can talk about it all you want, but if you aren't doing it, then it won't stick with the congregation. This should be something that you model by spending time with and really getting to know, care for, and empower a few individuals. As mentioned earlier, this could be your board of elders, your staff, your leadership team, or a few high-quality potential leaders. I strongly suggest that this group always include one or two persons in their teens or twenties. A structured intern program is a great way to include the younger generations. Finding students with high leadership potential, asking them to go through an application process, and having a plan of how you are going to invest in them over the course of the internship is powerful. It is worth a small investment from the church financially, and it helps develop future leaders to take the main roles. I recommend that all full-time staff have an intern or two. If a church with multiple staff members has interns, some of the training can be done together. It is a powerful way to invest intentionally, model a godly example, train in Scripture, and set up the future. (For a great example of a strong internship program in the youth area, check out www.internacademy.net.)

Another way to begin the shift toward a culture of spiritual formation is to have every main leader apprenticing or pouring into someone. For example, teachers should have another teacher that comes alongside of them, elders should have a possible future elder they are pouring into, and sound techs should have another sound tech they are pouring into. This helps create a culture of spiritual formation. Actually some secular organizations do this much better than the church. In technical fields, such as electricians, metal workers, and plumbers, there is a process of apprenticing someone to learn that trade. In the medical field, physicians have to come alongside older physicians and be apprenticed. It is a part of the culture. Wouldn't it be incredible if the church had that type of investment culture?

We have talked about church leaders and their investment in others, but what about helping everyone in the congregation become a part of the pass-the-baton culture? How can the vision move from the leadership core to everyone in your local congregation? First, remember it is a process and the leadership group will have to adapt and implement it among themselves for a time before it will start to catch on. It won't happen overnight. This isn't some great gimmick or "Five Ways to Grow Your Church" seminar. This is about cultural change, which takes time. However, the impact of this shift could last for generations.

I would suggest that the church leadership team begin to implement this pass-the-baton culture for six months or more before challenging the congregation and communicating the vision from the platform. The stories in the book of Judges and the failure of Joshua to pass the baton after the hand off from Moses is a great place to study to help those we lead understand the importance of passing the baton and the impact it will have on future generations. A theme for the year or season could be, "It just takes one," challenging all members to invest in their family members and one other person who is younger than they are over the next year. Since the leadership team has had some time to invest in others before this is made public, there should be some stories of the impact of passing the baton. There are all kinds of creative ways to keep this before members throughout the year with stories, videos, banners, updates, messages, and blogs.

For it to fully become a part of your culture, it will take more than talking about it during a six-week sermon series. To really develop a **GETS IT** culture, I would suggest having it as a major focus for at least a year, intertwining it throughout the life of the church. After that intense focus, having it become a part of the leadership culture, as well as keeping it before the congregation at least quarterly, will help maintain the priority of passing the baton.

Some words of caution: not everyone will be as excited about investing in others as you are. As we discussed earlier, fear often holds people back. Sometimes it is helpful to verbalize some of these possible fears as you challenge the congregation. We have to recognize that the enemy does not want us to build this into our DNA because of the impact it can have for eternity. If he can keep us focused on less important things, he can keep the church from having a generational impact. Just keep heading toward the goal and remember what is at stake.

It is also wise to realize that investing in others is often messy and can have its ups and downs. You or one of your leaders may invest in someone with all your heart and soul, only to have that person leave the church or abandon the faith. This can be very deflating. I have been there; but we must realize that it happens. Scripture shows that this happened to the apostle Paul and even to Jesus, so it's clearly not the mentor's inadequacies that cause it to happen. I remember some individuals that I poured my life into and then they went a different direction away from the faith. The thing that God reminds me of in these situations is that he is in control and the investment isn't void. Years later, God may gently use our earlier investment of time to speak to that individual's heart. Realize that passing the baton is a journey and there are often tough seasons along the way. Don't give up; the investment will make a difference. And God uses these times to develop us as much as the persons we are investing in. Most of all remember that it is worth it! The next generation is counting on us! When they write our story, my prayer is that they will say we were the church that handed off the baton of faith well to their generation.

Application Questions

1. On a scale of 1 to 10 (10 = "doing a great job"; 1 = "not at all"), how would you rank your local congregation in passing the baton of faith?

2. If you ranked your church below a 10, what are some things you could do to improve your discipling ministry?

3. How could you make sure that your church leaders live by the GETS IT principle?

4. You are called to invest your time and attention in many people, but who is someone you could personally disciple for Christ?

5. What two steps could you take in the next month to move your ministry team toward better implementing the GETS IT principle?

Chapter Ten

Race Victories

PRESENT-DAY STORIES OF BIBLICAL DISCIPLESHIP
Here we are at the last chapter of this book, but really it's just the beginning of the journey. Hopefully you have been challenged, encouraged, and motivated to commit to invest life on life in someone in a younger generation—to be a part of a movement that helps the next generation be one that **GETS IT**. My prayer is that you see the importance and the simplicity of living as a Godly Example, Training in Scripture, and investing Intentional Time in someone who is younger to hand off the baton of faith smoothly.

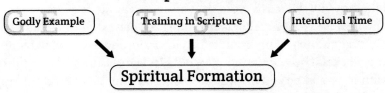

I was reminded of how important smooth hand offs are when I attended the funeral of my ninety-nine-year-old grandfather. What a life he lived. He was a great mentor to me, a godly man, a bivocational pastor for sixty-five years, and a man who lived everything I have written in this book. Much of my desire to invest in the younger generations is because of the baton he passed to me. Throughout his entire life he invested in the younger generations—teenagers and even elementary school kids. As a bivocational pastor who supplemented his income by painting houses, he would hire young kids and teenagers to help him. Most of those kids, myself included, usually caused more cleanup work for him than had he done it alone. We were often more trouble than help, and we were definitely overpaid, but he didn't do it for the work we produced; he did it for the chance to have life-on-life investments with eternal results. Frequently, the kids he invested in didn't have the best home life. In many cases, he may have been the only person who really believed in them. He would bring them to his church, take them to get ice cream, play baseball with them, and teach them the importance of work and how to use money. Yet more than that, he taught them how to know God.

My adopted brother was one of those kids. When my brother was eleven years old, my grandfather lived as a godly example, invested time in him, and helped him see life through Scripture. His home life was very rough. As the oldest child at eleven years old, he was responsible for his younger brothers, who were seven and four. He was responsible for feeding them, taking care of them, and making sure they made it to school and back. He said he would come home from school and his mom didn't care where he had been all day or even all night as long as he made it home to go to school the next morning. His parents would party all weekend, and they would often take him with them. His mom and dad abused all kinds of substances, and he was exposed to things at a young age that no child should see. Through the help of my grandfather, my mom and dad adopted him when he was twelve years old. Now decades later, he has a relationship with Jesus and he and his wife are trying to help their two children live God's plan for them. The baton was passed.

When I think of the investment others have made in my life, I could write pages and pages and I would still leave someone out. I have had and still have so many individuals who believe in me and have poured themselves into me. My parents were incredible examples of the **GETS IT** process. I could write an entire chapter detailing how they lived as godly examples, trained us in Scripture, and invested intentional time in me and my siblings when we were growing up and now after we are all grown and have families. I mentioned my brother above; my sister is raising her family in Oklahoma, where she is a youth pastor. Both sets of my grandparents lived the spiritual formation equation and passed the baton well. I have had the passing of the baton modeled for four generations, which I believe has helped give me much insight into and appreciation of the process.

There were numerous other individuals who believed in the discipleship process and who invested in me. I am not even going to attempt to list all the influencers for fear of leaving someone out—from older regular mentors who have taken time to sit across the table from me helping me process life, to those who have been in my life for short seasons or just for a time or two. When I reflect on the people who invested in my life and my spiritual formation process, I see that it often occurred during life-on-life interactions. I often think of the people who believed in me and those who invested in me. Those who spoke encouraging words and said things like, "You can do ," "I believe in you," "You are going to make a difference," always spurred me on. Even today, from time to time, I still think about encouraging words spoken years ago, and they help me keep moving forward.

I thought it would be beneficial for you to hear stories from others of how God has used people to make a difference in their lives. I hope these stories challenge you, encourage you, and spark ideas of how you can pass the baton and be a part of the **GETS IT** movement.

STEVE'S STORY

There is no doubt in my mind that I would not be where I am today, doing what I am doing, if not for godly people pouring into my life and modeling a life of generosity, grace, leadership, balance, and passion. I am the product of words such as "I believe in you" and "God has big plans for you." Phrases like these have sculpted my life. Ken Love once said that "words create worlds." I feel like I was the recipient of godly people opening up new worlds to me. Looking back, some of my heroes are people who took risks on me that I am not sure I would have taken on myself. To this day, I am able to live and lead with a greater level of confidence and significance because of the people who handed off the baton to me.

JEANNETTE'S STORY

To a large extent each of us is the product of those who were willing to invest in mentoring us, training us, and giving us opportunities to experience and learn. My life and ministry have been shaped by the gift of time leaders gave me and who taught me by their conversation and message. I value deeply those who were patient enough and cared enough to coach and train me in how to be more effective in specific ways. But even more formative were those men and women who believed in God's call on my life so much that they gave me the freedom and opportunity to test my naïve ideas, explore new ministry methods, and were still there to support and encourage me when I failed. One of the deepest lessons and greatest gifts my mentors gave to me was their model of unbridled love and passion for fulfilling the mission of our Savior. The mentors who placed their hands and prayers on my life certainly changed me by their wisdom, their skill, their affirmation, and the amazing grace they gave as I learned to stumble, walk, run, and soar in the calling of God. But the mentors who influenced me most clearly were those men and women who were not just interested in giving me knowledge, skill or ability, but who loved me because they loved the kingdom so greatly!

WES'S STORY

If you have ever watched a relay race in the Olympics, you have seen the very intentional way that a runner passes the baton. Once the runner crosses a certain line, both he and the next runner begin to run in sequence until the first runner finally hands over the baton. This is a perfect picture of the way that I was discipled through high school and how I continued to be discipled in college. Those key people who have poured into my life over the years never just tossed me the baton and expected me to win the race, nor did they tell me to stand on the sidelines while they ran the race. They carried the responsibility and the pressure but asked me to run with them. They asked me to worship with them, to preach with them, to plan with them, to pray with them, and to share life with them. Discipleship is about giving someone the chance to really run, to try new things and experiment with new ideas, to fall down and get back up, to fail, to succeed, to become frustrated, and to do all these things confidently with the understanding that though they could receive the baton any minute, they do not yet hold it. Discipleship is that beautiful window in time when the fresh runner steadies himself for the race ahead by matching strides with those who have already been running.

TAMI'S STORY

The people God has provided as my mentors and coaches have been uniquely fitted for each season of my life. I remember the thirtysomething single youth leader who gave me a ride to youth meeting each week when I was a young teen. As we were driving to our destination, she showed genuine concern about what was happening in my life and often talked about what strengths and gifts she saw in me. I think about my Sunday school teacher in high school and college who encouraged me and believed in me, even when he saw me at my worst. I fondly remember my now deceased mentor, Anita, who invested regularly in my life and ministry as I went through the ordination process. I recall the way the senior pastor at my first ministry assignment gave me freedom to make decisions and backed me up—even when I made mistakes as a young youth pastor. The common factors in each of these relationships were their investment of time, their belief in me, and their confidence that God had a plan for my life. These things affirmed me and encouraged me to seek God's will in my life and ministry.

KRISTI'S STORY

When I think of the time I was most spiritually renewed and connected, it was when someone else was pouring into my life on a consistent basis. When I was newly married, I was fortunate enough to have a woman older than myself mentor me weekly. We met one morning a week and she would listen and give me spiritual wisdom. She was someone who motivated me to love Jesus more and made me want to be more like him. Every week at Barnes and Noble we would delve into a Bible study or share our hearts with one another.

She herself was also being poured into on a weekly basis by a mentor, and this weekly consistent contact helped me grow closer to God and helped me give my all to God.

ERIC'S STORY

I am eternally grateful for those who have been mentors in my life. The power of positive investment has helped me throughout life. As I think about the people who have poured into my life through the years, I think about people who spoke positive words of belief into my life and future, and I think about people who encouraged me with prayer and intentional statements, such as "You can do it," "I believe in you," and "There is no doubt that God has his hand on your life." I can't express how valuable these people have been. One of the greatest ways that mentors have discipled me is by modeling a lifestyle that is Christ-centered and full of integrity. The power of positive investment in my life growing up and even today has been incredible. I realize the value of having people in my life that are speaking belief, value, truth, and wisdom. I believe that the mentors in my life are people that God has used to help me grow and develop as a child, teenager, young adult, and even today. I praise God daily for these individuals.

CHELSIE'S STORY

A big part of my development and growth has come from the leaders I have served with as a part of a student leadership team. They have pushed me to be a Christ-centered leader and to live a life for Christ daily. They have taught me the importance of being a strong Christian leader among my peers, as well as being courageous in standing up for my values. They are really encouraging and want the best for me and everyone else on the team. They take the time to get to know me, pray for me, and love me. When my sister was sick, they prayed, called, and e-mailed me to show that they really cared. At other times, I just needed someone to talk to about what was going on in my life and they were always there. We stay in touch through Facebook, e-mail, and phone calls. They have all had a huge impact on my life. When I am in ministry, I want to be able to influence a person's life just as much as they have influenced mine.

RYAN'S STORY

Three things stand out to me as major reasons for our faith and ministry development in my local church as a student. The first was the unusually high degree of belief in us and in our contributions. We were communicated to with the highest respect, and whatever we did was always spoken of as outstanding. Second, we were given opportunities to serve. These opportunities were not relegated to junior church or youth ministries but were right in the mix with the adults. Third, although we were far younger, we were considered equal partners with older church leaders. There was no condescension because of our age. We were valued as much as anyone else. This sense of importance was spoken into us in so many ways and by so many people in the life of the congregation that it paved the way for many of us to become kingdom leaders.

ANNE'S STORY

With a simple hug or a word of kindness, my family, friends, and church members have always been there to remind me to seek God, trust God, love God, and share God. They have encouraged me from the talents God has given them, through their smiles in times of joy and through their tears in times of pain. They walk beside me in this dark world and remind me to shine with God's love in everything I do. With so many people being examples of Christ to me, I hope it is contagious! I hope people will see Christ's love in me and I will be an encouragement to others, and that this contagious thing called God's love will go on and on!

ARTHUR'S STORY

My teaching mentor was Harry. Let me take you back to the start of our relationship. My entry into teaching was casual. I was entering the end of my undergraduate career and recently married when I suddenly realized that I was going to have to do something with this degree to support a marriage. I thought: "I like school. I'll be a teacher." That settled it. I went to graduate school, earned certification, and was employed as an English teacher in Red Bluff, California. There Harry came into my life. He was the sophomore class counselor, and nearly everything I did affecting sophomores had to go through him. One requirement was "cinch" notices; these blue cards had to be delivered to the counselor for all students who, at a given point, were a "cinch" to fail. So, as a new teacher wanting to do the right thing, I filled out cinch notices for at least one-third of my students and dutifully walked them over to Harry. One look and he said, "Let's talk." That "Let's talk" was the beginning of a lifelong relationship that became a strong friendship but was always about mentoring. Through his experiential wisdom and thoughtful counsel, I discovered what really matters about teaching and managed my way through the often deadening bureaucracy of public schools.

What did Harry do? He asked questions. The first one was, "Do you really want to process these?" My response: "I thought I had to." "Well," Harry said, "let's take a look." At the end of that conversation, two things had happened: that one-third was reduced to 1% and I had a wise mentor. For years, Harry and I talked about what really matters in teaching and how to be an effective teacher. I discovered along the line that the casual decision I made was really a God-decision and that my own God-gift was teaching. What Harry did for me, other than be a true friend, was by example, question, and precept, to hone, sharpen, and focus my gift so that I could pierce through the unessential and address what is fundamentally at the heart of teaching—developing relationships between students and teacher in which living well is finally what learning is about, no matter the subject.

BRITTANY'S STORY

Some people who have invested in my life are my family and my church family. I come from a Christian family that has always taught me to love God. Seeing my parents live their lives for God made me, at an early age, want that life too. My family has also taught me to believe in myself and that I can accomplish anything that I put my mind to. My church family has also invested in my life. They have invested in me financially and spiritually. Through fundraisers to go to youth conventions or other church-related activities, they always helped make a way. Certain people from my church showed me how to live my life for Christ by being active in the church to bring glory to God. The older individuals, especially, through their life experiences have shown me not to give up during the tough times. Now, I am an influence to the youth and younger children in the church. Without my family or church, I wouldn't be the loving Christian woman that I am today.

ARLO'S STORY

Every life needs a landmark, something by which to determine direction, to measure distance, and to evaluate decisions being made. Such a landmark does not control your actions but remains steadfast, enabling you to determine the direction you will take and the results of such action. Like a lighthouse, it doesn't force you; it only makes you aware of your surroundings.

Beyond the spiritual landmarks of my godly parents, there have been key persons whom I have observed and from whom I have learned as examples of a balanced Christian ministry. The late Dr. Kardatzke was and continues to be such a mentor, a landmark that has remained solid across some sixty years. I had just been discharged from the U.S. Navy and as a high school dropout was attempting to find myself and my place in God's work. I visited a church camp where the guest conference leader was Carl Kardatzke, professor of education at Anderson College. We became friends and spent time discussing life in the post-war world of 1946. No, he did not enroll me in college; he listened and then made me aware of GED tests and the GI bill.

My decision to enter college that fall continued this mentoring relationship, preparing me for marriage and ministry. When I needed counsel, he was a good listener, sometimes challenging the direction being considered and at other times calling me to accountability; but he was always the same, a true landmark. Dr. Kardatzke has been gone for many years, yet I follow his example of faithful Christian ministry, wanting to finish well as he did.[1]

JOSHUA'S STORY

In the past twenty-two years of my life, there have been many who have contributed to my life. In fact, I'm under the opinion that everyone I've ever come into contact with has changed me in some way. The people who really stand out from that group with the biggest influence in my life are those who intentionally spent time and effort to invest in me. I can name about ten people who consistently poured into my life. I want to tell you about one in particular. His name is Pastor Ken. We laughed together, cried together, served together, and prayed together. One of the most influential aspects of our relationship was that he was real with me. Ken shared with me the truth about who he was and where he had come from. We talked about struggles, joys, fears, and hopes. His openness allowed me to feel free to share things about my life that I wouldn't share with just anyone. He was always quick to listen and slow to talk. Often he wouldn't try to give me answers but would direct me to ask better questions. Ken is a man who I now pattern my life after because he showed me so clearly who and whose he is and forever will be.

ASHLEY'S STORY

Those who have invested in me have been persistent and intentional. They asked tough questions and let me know it was okay to answer them because they listened without an agenda. They gave me their time and in return only expected my company. Something as little as inquiring about how a test went or asking about my family made a huge impact—not because they were asking, but because they genuinely wanted to know the answer. The people who have poured into my life believed in me and expressed it daily until I couldn't help but believe in myself as well. Investing in someone is not a onetime

---

1. This was written when Arlo was eighty-two as he was helping to pass the baton he has been handed by being a mentor in the author's life.

occurrence; it is an ongoing process of caring for someone so much that you give of yourself selflessly.

MARK'S STORY

I have a long legacy of people who invested in me. My grandparents would include me in their antiquing on Saturdays, and I watched their every move, watching how they treated each other and how much they loved what they did. My mom taught me a great work ethic and my dad taught me tremendous people skills. My church family looked after me and gave me many examples to follow. My youth pastor took me with him when he would go out to speak, and my pastor took me with him to meetings that he had to attend and took time to prepare me for the future beyond my small town in southeast Missouri. In college, it was my missions and anthropology professor who would take time out to invest in me, as well as my sociology professor, who helped me to dream and fall in love with the classroom. When my wife and I were about to get married, it was a retired neighbor couple who spoke into our lives. If you ever see a turtle on a fence post, you know it did not get there by itself, and that is my story!

JOSH'S STORY

I seem to thrive off two things: being encouraged and accomplishing difficult tasks. I found this to be a great combination for the athletic world, although it extends beyond athletics. I have always had an itch to get better, lead, and be a positive example while having the confidence that I could do so. However, I have found that confidence is not something that always comes from within. Failure overshadows success in many situations. I have found that confidence comes by means of encouragement, success, and the shared stories from those who have been through similar experiences.

Through the years I have had an amazing support group, including my youth pastor Ricky, my mom, dad, and grandparents. Ricky is a man that stands out to me because he invested in me beyond Sunday and Wednesday nights. While I was seeking out Christ, Ricky was looking to make a personal connection with me by taking me fishing, asking me to tackle projects with him, and having me over for dinner. Although I cannot remember all the things Ricky has said to me over the years, I do know that when Ricky spoke, it was always positive and encouraging when talking about life tasks. Ricky gave me the courage to encourage my own parents who did not know Christ or attend church to start attending with me. My parents now have given their lives to Christ and are active youth counselors in the church. During the time that I spent with Ricky, he would say things like "God has a great plan for your life," giving me the confidence and courage to go into full-time vocational ministry. I can only thank God for leading me to a man who had enough confidence in me to encourage me to have confidence in God's faithfulness and my God-given abilities even though he was not obligated to.

CHRISTIN'S STORY

Over the years, there have been people in my life who spoke truth to me, revealing to me through their actions who Jesus really is. I couldn't imagine my spiritual journey without them; I am blessed to even now have them as a part of my life. They encouraged me to grow in my faith and walked alongside me when I needed guidance and wisdom. They led small groups throughout middle school and high school, attended my basketball games and awards ceremonies, and made random phone calls and sent notes that seemed to come just at the right time. I couldn't say thank you enough to these people in my life, because they have helped shape who I am today.

Sometimes we get so caught up in the programs and doing big things, but really it comes down to the small stuff. Words such as "I am so proud of you," "I believe in you," and "God has amazing things in store for you" still ring loudly in my ears and do far more than any message from a platform ever could. Those who invest in the lives of others will no doubt face tiring times, but from someone who couldn't have made it without them, never give up. Your work is doing amazing things for the kingdom of God and the fruits of your labor are blessing more than you know. What you do matters!

These stories are just a sampling of the influence that individuals have who are a part of the **GETS IT** movement—people who believed in the process of being Godly examples, helping to direct others in Scripture, and intentionally investing time in others. With God's help and his Spirit, the baton was passed well. What are people going to write about you? What are they going to write about us as a Christian community? My prayer is that you become a part of the **GETS IT** movement by starting today in investing in someone younger than you and setting yourself up to pass off the baton well. No matter what our age, fourteen or eighty, God has given us a baton to pass. When the history books write the final conclusion for our generation, may they say, "Everyone did as God instructed them and the generations that followed sought after God."

Application Questions

1. As you read the stories of smooth hand offs, whose story made the deepest impression on you? Why?

2. Were you surprised by any of the stories? Why?

3. What themes seemed to run through all of the stories?

4. Tell the story of someone who really made a difference in your spiritual life. What did they do?

5. Your family is your first priority for passing the baton of faith. Identify at least one person outside your family with whom you will share your faith. What steps are you taking to do that?

Appendix
Resources to get you started

FOR AGES 12 AND UNDER
A great bible story book is *Egermeier's Bible Story Book*. This is available from Warner Press (www.warnerpress.org). There are also other good children's books available on this site.
The *Jesus Storybook Bible* is another great storybook that you can find at a Christian bookstore or at Amazon.com

FOR TEENAGERS AND COLLEGE STUDENTS
Bibles: There are many youth Bibles on the market today. I would suggest getting one that has study helps and is in an easy to read translation, such as the New Living Translation (NLT) or the New Century Version (NCV)
Great study books for guys: *Every Young Man's Battle* by Stephen Arterburn and Fred Stoeker, published by Waterbrook Press.
Great study books for girls: *Every Young Woman's Battle* by Shannon Ethridge and Stephen Arterburn, published by Waterbrook Press.

FOR BOTH GENDERS:
The Ultimate Adventure Remix series is a four level discipleship curriculum distinctive in its approach to experiential learning, opportunities to live out our faith, and leadership development. For more information, visit www.chogy.org and click on the resource tab.
The Case for Christ, student edition, by Lee Strobel and Jane Vogel, published by Zondervan.
The Case for Faith, student edition, by Lee Strobel and Jane Vogel, published by Zondervan.
Experiencing God, youth edition, by Henry T. Blackaby and Claude V. King, published by Lifeway Christian Resources.

FOR ADULTS

Bibles: There are many bibles on the market today. I would suggest getting one that has study helps and is in an easy to read translation, such as the New Living Translation (NLT) or the New Century Version (NCV)

Great study books for men: *Every Man's Battle* by Stephen Arterburn and Fred Stoeker, published by Waterbrook Press.

Great study books for women: *Every Woman's Battle* by Shannon Ethridge and Stephen Arterburn, published by Waterbrook Press.

FOR BOTH GENDERS:

The Case for Christ, by Lee Strobel and Jane Vogel, published by Zondervan.

The Case for Faith, by Lee Strobel and Jane Vogel, published by Zondervan.

Experiencing God, by Henry T. Blackaby and Claude V. King, published by Lifeway Christian Resources.

Application Questions

1. Name someone [illegible] In what [illegible]

2. Dr. Stephenson notes that [illegible]

CPSIA information can be obtained
at www.ICGtesting.com
Printed in the USA
FFOW04n1002140218
45100188-45513FF

9 781593 175931